IN WHOSE IMAGE?

To my mother, Eva Louise Hickerson,
and
my father, Henry Truman Aldredge,
whose love led me to believe in the love
of a Mother and Father God

IN WHOSE IMAGE?
God and Gender

Jann Aldredge Clanton

CROSSROAD • NEW YORK

1991

The Crossroad Publishing Company
370 Lexington Avenue, New York, NY 10017

Copyright © 1990 by Jann Aldredge Clanton

Printed in the United States of America

Library of Congress Cataloging-in-Publication Data

Clanton, Jann Aldredge, 1946-
    In whose image? : God and gender / Jann Aldredge Clanton.
      p. cm.
    Bibliography: p.
    Includes index,
    ISBN 0-8245-1031-3
    1. Femininity of God. 2. Transcendence of God. I. Title.
BT153.M6C42   1989
231'.4 — dc20
                                   89-40242
                                     CIP

Contents

Acknowledgements   vii

Introduction   1

1 The Bible and How We Read It   5
   God-Breathed Word   6
   Passing Down the Word   11
   Interpreting the Word 14
   Questions for Discussion   18

2 The Unlimited God of Scripture   20
   In the Beginning 21
   Other Old Testament Pictures of God   23
   New Testament Images   29
   Questions for Discussion   37

3 How We Got Where We Are   38
   The Early Church 40
   The Middle Ages   43
   The Reformation 46
   The Modern Church   50
   Questions for Discussion   54

4 Models of Change: If God Can Include Three Persons,
   Can't God Include Two Genders?   55
   Heresy Then and Now 56
   Beyond Heresy   62
   Questions for Discussion   65

5 God-Language and Self-Esteem in Women   **66**
     When God Is More Than Man   69
     When God Is Man   72
     Freeing the Spirit Within Women   76
     Questions for Discussion   80

6 God-Language and Spirituality in Men   **81**
     The Price Men Pay   82
     God Beyond Man   84
     Freeing the Spirit Within Men   90
     Questions for Discussion   94

7 God-Language and the Church's Future   **95**
     Gender of God and of God's Ministers   96
     When God and Humanity Are Liberated   98
     Questions for Discussion 106

Epilogue: Beyond God as Male and Female   **107**

Appendix A: Religious Opinion Survey   **111**

Appendix B: Statistical Analysis of *t* Tests   **116**

Notes   **117**

Inclusive Language Resources for the Church   **127**

Index of Scripture References   **129**

General Index   **133**

Acknowledgements

My genuine appreciation goes to those men and women who helped me give birth to this book. My husband, David, gave primary assistance with his editorial comments, technical expertise in the production of graphs and manuscripts, and loving encouragement and support. My sister, Dr. Anne Morton, gave valuable help in the choosing of instruments for the psychological research and in the interpretation of the results, while inspiring my confidence throughout the process. My friend and colleague in ministry, Rev. Dr. Elizabeth Bellinger, added keen editorial insight and overall support for the project. Dr. Roger Kirk and graduate students Rebecca Buchanan and Barbara Foster, from the Behavioral Statistics Department of Baylor University, did the statistical analyses.

I am especially grateful to the 174 women and men in my research sample, and to John Eagleson and Pamela Johnson at Meyer-Stone Books. The creativity and encouragement of my sons, Chad and Brett, continually bless my life and work.

Introduction

Is woman in the image of God? Genesis 1:27 states that she is, but that has not stopped some theologians from denying that she is. Christian history is filled with pronouncements and debates on the "woman question." What many interpreters have failed to realize is that the "woman question" is also the "man question," and ultimately a "God question." If woman, like man, is made in the image of God, then God's image includes the feminine as well as the masculine, and men and women stand in equal partnership.

We need more inclusive understandings of God if equality between the sexes is to become reality in church and society. If we can conceive a God who includes and transcends both masculine and feminine, we will grow in our experience of God and humanity. As the church stretches beyond exclusive masculine images of God, we will increase our understanding of God and ourselves, awakening to our power and potential. Tom Neufer Emswiler testifies to the growth he experienced through expanding his language for God:

> It has not only sensitized me to the concerns of women but also to those of many other oppressed groups. The revolution in language that I have experienced in my talk about God has had more influence on the growth of my theological understanding than any other factor. It has deepened my theological insight and my spiritual life.[1]

As the church moves into the twenty-first century, we struggle to proclaim timeless truth in a dramatically changing world. God calls us to re-examine our beliefs and make our practice consistent, so that we can speak the gospel of peace and justice in

1

our world today. The church awaits a renewal that will come as we expand our understanding of God. Although we can never describe the experience of the Transcendent, our attempts toward a doctrine of God (formal statement of belief) form the foundation for our faith and practice.

In 1958, J. B. Phillips proclaimed that our "God is too small." We try to tame and limit God to fit our comprehension. Phillips states that the chief cause of the decline of some churches is the worship of an inadequate god, a cramped and regulated god. Many people have not found a God large enough for modern needs. While their experience of life has grown and their mental horizons have expanded, their ideas of God have remained largely static.[2] Today Phillips's words are still all too true.

Awakenings within the church have come when Christians have opened their minds and spirits, allowing God to be who God will be. Expanded concepts of God allow the fresh breath of the Spirit to move through the church. The church today stands ready to move beyond exclusive masculine concepts of God. A masculine god is an inadequate god. Exclusive masculine images of God stifle the full development and contributions of females and males within the church. This narrow concept of God enslaves the church to patriarchal culture. When the church liberates God from exclusive masculine language, members will be free to become what God created, and the church will be free to be an agent of transformation.

My study takes Scripture seriously. It begins with a discussion of biblical inspiration, translation, and interpretation. Then I survey the variety of ways the Bible pictures God. Limiting God by masculine language ignores parts of God's revelation. From various interpretations of Scripture, Christian theologians down through the centuries have attempted to describe God. Looking at some of these descriptions, which include "Christ Mother" and "the womb of God the Father," will help us see how we got where we are today. Then taking the church's struggle toward a doctrine of the Trinity as a model, I suggest ways the church can develop gender-inclusive images of God.

This book moves on to explore relationships between concepts of God and concepts of self. Theology has psychological implications. The way we imagine God affects the way we feel about ourselves and the way we relate to one another within the church. When we limit our thinking and speaking about God to masculine images, females and males fail to realize their full potential. Women become handicapped by lack of confidence and unhealthy dependence. Men become burdened by excessive responsibility and impoverished in their spirituality. Thus the entire church is stunted.

Balanced, inclusive understandings of God result in greater wholeness of both women and men. With a concept of God as female and male, men and women come to a deeper realization of themselves as created in God's image. Then women and men become free to develop their leadership and spiritual potential, and the church is enriched and expanded. Inclusive images of God in worship bring individual and corporate growth and renewal. Challenging and expanding our limited concepts of God and of ourselves, Christ continues to "make all things new" (Rev. 21:5).

Chapter 1

The Bible and How We Read It

For my thoughts are not your thoughts, neither are your ways my ways, says the Lord. For as the heavens are higher than the earth, so are my ways higher than your ways and my thoughts than your thoughts. (Isa. 55:8–9)[1]

When I was a child in Vacation Bible School, I learned to sing a song about the Bible: "I know the Bible was sent from God, the Old as well as the New. Divinely inspired the whole way through, I know the Bible is true." After years of studying the Bible, I still hold the firm conviction that the Bible is the divinely inspired Word of God.

What does it mean to say that the Bible is divinely inspired? Once I believed this meant that God dictated every word verbatim. I accepted every part of the Bible as God's Word without question. My position was similar to that expressed in the popular bumper sticker: "God said it. I believe it. That settles it."

Then I came across the last verse of Psalm 137, which pronounces a blessing upon anyone who will take Babylonian babies and smash them against the rocks. I knew that the Babylonians had been cruel to the Israelites, God's chosen people. But Jesus said, "Love your enemies and pray for those who persecute you" (Matt. 5:44). How could two passages of Scripture with such opposite attitudes toward enemies both be the inspired Word of God? I had met the problem of biblical inspiration.

Growing up in Sunday School, I had a King James Version of the Bible with a red-leather cover and the words of Christ in red. I was proud of this Bible. In a missions organization for girls I memorized many passages of Scripture, all in the King James Version. Though I came to understand that the Revised Standard Version is a more accurate translation, I still love the poetry of the twenty-third Psalm in the King James Version. "Yea though I walk through the valley of the shadow of death" may not be as meaningful to modern ears as "Even though I walk through the valley of the shadow of death," but the former sounds more poetic to my ears.

Nonetheless, I appreciate many changes made in modern translations. When I used to read John 16:21 in the King James Version, I felt pain that a mother rejoiced because a *male* child was born. "A woman when she is in travail hath sorrow, because her hour is come: but as soon as she is delivered of the child, she remembereth no more the anguish, for joy that a man is born into the world." The Revised Standard reads "for joy that a child is born into the world." The Revised Standard is the more accurate translation because the Greek word here means "a human being," not "man." I had met the problem of biblical translation.

Once I questioned why women did not cover their heads in our church when the Bible says that we should. I got the answer, "Paul meant that passage only for the women back then because of that particular culture." Then I asked why there were no women pastors in my denomination. The answer came, "The Bible says that women are to be silent in the church." Later I discovered that the historical principle of biblical interpretation was being applied in the first instance and not in the second, even though both passages had the same historical setting in Corinth. I had met the problem of biblical interpretation.

God-Breathed Word

The Bible itself provides the primary source for our understanding of biblical inspiration. "All scripture is inspired by God" [*theopneustos*, which literally means "God-breathed"] (2 Tim. 3:16). When God inspired Paul to write these words, "Scripture" included only the Hebrew Bible.[2] The Gospels, Paul's epistles — the entire New Testament — had not yet been officially declared Scripture. Those who take the word "all" literally to support an inerrant view of the Bible must also take the term "Scripture" literally. This literalistic approach leads to the conclusion that God inspired only the Old Testament. But Scripture came not through a mechanical dictation process that we can examine under a microscope. Scripture came from the breath of God. Herein lies mystery, not logical explanation. The Bible sets forth no theory of inspiration by which it originated. The Bible says nothing about how the inspiration took place. The breath of God gave birth to it, just as the breath of God gave birth to the universe. Once Jesus encountered a man named Nicodemus, who wanted rational explanations for the work of God. Jesus compared the activity of God's Spirit to the wind that "blows where it wills, and you hear the sound of it, but you do not know whence it comes or whither it goes" (John 3:8). When we examine biblical revelation and inspiration, we seek some understanding of a mystery.

"Revelation" refers to the activity of God. It means God's unveiling or disclosure to us. Divine revelation comes through the Spirit: "God has revealed to us through the Spirit. For the Spirit searches everything, even the depths of God" (1 Cor. 2:10). When the Bible speaks of God's revelation, it does not mean that God allowed human beings to see God or know everything about God. Revelation is not a one-time, mechanical unveiling of God. In the Bible, revelation is God in action. The name for God in the Hebrew Bible is *YHWH*, an action word. *YHWH* is a verb form meaning "I am who I am," or "I will be who I will be." God will not be constricted by our limited understanding and our narrow categories. We understand something of God's nature through God's creative activity in the world and in the lives of human beings. God's action changes and progresses with people's capacity to understand.

God's revelation comes through the universe God created. Creation bears the marks of its Creator. "The heavens are telling the glory of God; and the firmament proclaims God's handiwork" (Ps. 19:1). Paul takes God's revelation through nature to mean that we are all accountable to God. "Ever since the creation of the world God's invisible nature, namely, God's eternal power and deity, has been clearly perceived in the things that have been made. So they are without excuse" (Rom. 1:20). God's revelation in nature and in history we call general revelation.

Particular revelation is God's disclosure through the written word, the Bible. God has spoken uniquely through biblical revelation. However, this does not mean every word in Scripture equally carries God's revelation. C. S. Lewis says that "all Holy Scripture is in some sense — though not all parts of it in the same sense — the word of God."[3] God's revelation in the psalms that pray curses upon enemies falls far short of that in the Sermon on the Mount in which Jesus teaches love of enemies. Christians believe that Jesus Christ is God's ultimate revelation. Christ serves as the divine standard by which we evaluate all Scripture.

Although God's revelation in Christ is complete, human understanding of this revelation is quite incomplete. God's revelation is ongoing in the sense that God continually discloses truth about the incarnation. Jesus realized that the disciples could understand only partial revelation. Shortly before leaving this earth, Jesus told the disciples, "I have yet many things to say to you, but you cannot bear them now" (John 16:12). Christ goes on to tell them that the Spirit of truth will guide them to deeper revelation. This Spirit still guides us today toward fuller understanding of God's revelation in Christ. This revelation unfolds and grows with each generation. For example, Jesus taught the worth of each individual equally created in God's image. It was this teaching of Christ that inspired Paul to write, "There is neither Jew nor Greek, there is neither slave nor free, there is neither male nor female; for you are all one in Christ Jesus" (Gal. 3:28). The first-century Christians struggled to break down the barriers between Jews and Gentiles. But not until the nineteenth century did Americans break the bonds that enslaved black people. And not until a generation ago did we pass civil rights laws to give black Americans equality. Our generation has yet to grasp fully God's revelation that "there is neither male nor female" in Christ Jesus. The Spirit is still in the process of revealing meanings and applications of the biblical revelation of Christ.

The Holy Spirit inspired those who recorded the message of redemption through Christ. The process by which the Spirit guided the minds of those who wrote the Bible we call "inspiration." God's inspiration of the biblical writers differs from the inspiration of great philosophers, artists, and musicians. But

God did not erase the human personality and the culture of the writers of the Bible.

The mechanical dictation theory of biblical inspiration assumes that the biblical writers were totally passive scribes with God dictating every word. This view denies the human element in the Bible. It takes only a close reading of the Gospels to see the influence of the author's personality upon the accounts. The author of Mark, for example, writes concise, fast-moving prose. The author of Matthew goes into more detail to prove the Messiahship of Jesus to the Jews. And if God dictated every word, it is hard to explain minor inconsistencies. For example, 2 Samuel 10:18 says that David killed the Syrians of 700 chariots, while the parallel account in 1 Chronicles 19:18 says that David killed the Syrians of 7,000 chariots.

The verbal plenary theory of biblical inspiration holds that every book of the Bible is equally inspired and that this inspiration applies to every kind of knowledge encountered in the Bible. Thus the Bible contains no errors in history, science, philosophy, or any other field of knowledge. Although this view takes seriously the divine element in the Bible, it overlooks some obvious human errors. For example, Mark 2:26 says that David "entered the house of God when Abiathar was high priest." However 1 Samuel 21 records that Ahimelech, not Abiathar, was high priest when David was fleeing from Saul. Matthew 27:5 and Acts 1:18 give conflicting accounts of Judas's death. Matthew records that Judas hanged himself, and Acts records that Judas fell on the ground and "burst open in the middle and all his bowels gushed out." If we hold a view of the Bible as inerrant, we have to do mental gymnastics to try to reconcile such historical inconsistencies.

To believe in the inspiration of the Bible we do not need to believe that originally there had to be a letter-perfect manuscript. The dynamic theory of biblical inspiration understands the Bible to be a reliable account of God's redemptive work. This view emphasizes the message of God's salvation more than the method or process by which it was put in written form. The dynamic view focuses on the function of the Bible to change lives more than the explanation of the process of inspiration. Scripture is a "God-breathed" miracle. We cannot fully explain "whence it comes." When we view inspiration as dynamic, we can see the unfolding, progressive nature of revelation that arises from the realities of human history and reaches its fullness in Jesus Christ.

When God inspired the biblical writers, God did not violate their freedom as persons. No matter how much we think God should have cut the biblical writers free from the prejudices and limitations of their culture, this is not what God chose to do. C. S. Lewis says that the "human qualities of the raw materials show through. Naivety, error, contradiction, even (as in the cursing Psalms) wickedness are not removed."[4]

The cultural prejudices of the biblical writers show through the biblical revelation. The Jewish psalmist prayed God's wrath upon Gentile nations (Ps. 79:6). Some Jewish Christians in the early church stubbornly insisted that Gentiles must first become circumcised Jews before they could be saved (Acts 15:1). Though Paul knew Christ's message of the equal worth of all persons, Paul nevertheless reflected his own culture which condoned slavery. Thus he counsels slaves to be obedient to their masters (Eph. 6:5).

The Bible reflects the strong bias of a patriarchal (male-dominated) culture. Males dominated family and society. Only adult males could achieve full membership in the Jewish religious community. In Israelite culture women were totally dependent on their fathers and husbands even in religious matters. A father or husband could veto a woman's religious vows (Num. 30:3-15). Women had no rights of inheritance if there were male heirs (Num. 27:1-11). Women received harsher sentences for adultery than men (Num. 5:11-31). Jewish oral tradition declared that the testimony of one hundred women was not equal to that of one man. It is clear that the predominant culture of the biblical writers placed greater value on males than on females. Thus the writers of the Bible refer to God as "he," even though the first word for God in the Bible includes masculine and feminine, and the word for Spirit throughout the Old Testament is feminine (Gen. 1:1-2).[5] The strict monotheism of the Jews kept them from using a plural pronoun for God. It is not surprising that they chose a masculine rather than a feminine singular pronoun for God. In that culture the way to give God the greatest honor and respect was to refer to God as masculine. Different cultures and different generations have differing

ways of showing respect. As a sign of respect, previous generations addressed God as "Thou" and "Thee" in their prayers.
Now most people believe they can address God as "You" without being disrespectful. In ancient Greek culture a way of paying
tribute to winners of athletic contests was to place laurel wreaths
upon their heads. Today the winners in the Olympic games receive medals.

The biblical revelation makes clear that Christ placed equal
value upon females and males. In our day the Spirit is leading
us toward deeper understanding and application of this truth.
Jesus referred to God as masculine because his Jewish disciples,
steeped in their male-dominated culture, could not bear fuller
revelation at that time (John 16:12). In our culture, which places
greater value on females, we can understand the Spirit's leading
us beyond referring to God as "he." We will be truer to the
inspired redemptive message of the Bible as we learn to call
God "she" as well as "he."

Passing Down the Word

Most of us do not read the Bible in the original languages of
Hebrew, Aramaic, and Greek. We have to rely upon translators.
Down through Christian history God has used translators to put
the biblical message into language that people could understand.
Translators have passed down God's Word by changing words
from the original languages into language that communicates to
wide varieties of people.

Throughout history people have met translations of the Bible
with strong resistance. Around A.D. 384 Jerome translated the
Bible from Greek and Hebrew into Latin, which had become
the language of the people in the church. Although this was a
clearer, more accurate translation, for a long time many people
preferred the Old Latin Versions. In 1382 John Wycliffe published the first complete Bible translated into English. Wycliffe
had a deep commitment to putting the biblical message into
the language of the common people so that they could study it
for themselves. But the religious authorities did not welcome
his translation. They condemned the Wycliffe Bible as heretical,
confiscated and burned copies of the Bible, and exhumed and
burned Wycliffe's body. William Tyndale's influential English

translation of 1525 likewise met strong ecclesiastical opposition. The church leaders strangled and burned Tyndale at the stake. In 1611 King James I of England authorized a team of Anglican scholars to make an English translation of the Bible. This King James Version initially met vigorous resistance from the bishops and the laypeople. In this century the Revised Standard Version and other modern translations more reliable than the King James Version came along. But not everyone has welcomed these new translations. Some people still say, "The King James Version was good enough for Jesus, and it's good enough for me." Believing that God spoke in King James English, they think modern translations are not as truly the Word of God.

It is sad then, though not surprising, that people today resist inclusive language translations of the Bible. The purpose of such translations is to communicate the biblical message in a way that is more consistent with our theology of a God transcending male and female and that frees human beings to become all God intended. For many years the strong criticism received by the National Council of Churches has slowed down progress toward an inclusive language translation. Today we hear accusations against inclusive language translations, accusations of tampering with the sacred text, of changing the Word of God. The King James Version and other translations also struggled in the midst of such accusations.

In 1983 the National Council of the Churches of Christ published *An Inclusive Language Lectionary*. The stated purpose of this inclusive language translation of biblical materials is as follows:

All persons are equally loved, judged, and accepted by God. This belief has been promoted by the church and has its roots in the origins of the Judeo-Christian tradition. Young and old, male and female, and persons of every racial, cultural, and national background are included in the faith community. Basic to a sense of equality and inclusiveness is the recognition that God by nature transcends all categories. God is more than male or female, and is more than can be described in historically and culturally limiting terms. God's holiness and mystery are present in the biblical tradition even if the words used to describe

God reflect limitations — words and language convey as best they can what is virtually impossible to describe.

Seeking to express the truth about God and about God's inclusive love for all persons, the Division of Education and Ministry of the National Council of Churches of Christ authorized the preparation of *An Inclusive Language Lectionary*.[6]

Although we love and cherish the translations we now use because of their familiarity, these translations are not totally accurate. Just as the writers of the original biblical texts lived in a male-biased culture, so the majority of biblical translators reflect the masculine bias of their society. For example, the Greek word *anthropos*, usually translated "man" in English Bibles, actually means "human being." In the original Hebrew, Deuteronomy 32:18 pictures God as a mother who gave birth to the Israelites. The King James Version does not accurately translate this feminine image of God: "Of the Rock that begat thee thou art unmindful, and hast forgotten God that formed thee." The Revised Standard Version comes closer to the Hebrew wording: "You were unmindful of the Rock that begot you, and you forgot the God who gave you birth."[7] Most glaring is the male bias of the translation in the Jerusalem Bible: "You forget the Rock who begot you, unmindful now of the God who fathered you."

Even though we know intellectually that the masculine language in the Bible comes from a culture limited by prejudice, we may feel comfortable with this language and want to hold on to it. We are used to hearing at the end of a wedding ceremony: "What therefore God has joined together, let not man put asunder" (Matt. 19:6). However, many ministers now say, "let no one put asunder." This translation more accurately reflects the original Greek, and more clearly communicates the message that no human being, man or woman, should break the bond between husband and wife.

New translations of the Bible threaten the security we feel with the familiar and challenge us to examine our theology. Thus our first inclination is to resist changes, just as people down through the ages have resisted new translations. But archaeologists and linguists continue to increase our knowledge of biblical culture and language. Today's translators can more accurately

convey the original message of the Bible than the translators of
the King James Version. The translators of the Revised Standard Version give two reasons for their new translation: (1) The
King James Version "contained the accumulated errors of four-
teen centuries of manuscript copying"; (2) English usage has
changed since 1611.

Today we have these same two compelling reasons for inclusive language translations of the Bible. Other translations
contain errors resulting from the masculine bias of the translators. English usage continues to move toward greater inclusiveness. Today school children learn to use "he or she" to refer
to a person and to say "people," not "men." Modern grammar
texts teach inclusive language, and major publishers now require
it. The translators of the Revised Standard Version wrote in
the Preface that the Word of God "must not be disguised in
phrases that are no longer clear, or hidden under words that have
changed or lost their meaning. It must stand forth in language
that is direct and plain, and meaningful to people today."[8]

Today the masculine language of most biblical translations
hides the true meaning of the words. This masculine language
confuses the meaning of the text and brings pain to many people
who feel excluded by it. It may not be comfortable and convenient for us to accept new inclusive language translations. These
translations will not gain immediate popularity. But following
God's Truth never has been easy or popular. We should use inclusive language in our churches because it best communicates
God's truth and promotes justice for all people.

Interpreting the Word

In 1984 the Southern Baptist Convention passed a resolution
against the ordination of women. A literal interpretation of
1 Timothy 2:11-12 prompted this resolution: "Let a woman
learn in silence with all submissiveness. I permit no woman to
teach or to have authority over men; she is to keep silent." Not
included in this resolution, however, was the preceding statement forbidding women to wear braided hair, gold, pearls, or
costly attire (1 Tim. 2:9), and the succeeding statement that
"woman will be saved through bearing children" (1 Tim. 2:15).
Those voting for this resolution against women's ordination

would say, "I believe the Bible is literally true." However, they chose only a few verses from this passage to take literally. So what they really mean is, "I believe that those portions of the Bible that I believe are literally true are literally true." Such selective literalism violates contextual and historical principles of biblical interpretation.

Down through history people have used the Bible to support the status quo, no matter how oppressive that may be. In the late nineteenth century Elizabeth Cady Stanton wrote, "When those who are opposed to all reforms can find no other argument, their last resort is the Bible. It has been interpreted to favor intemperance, slavery, capital punishment and the subjection of women." Many interpreters today still use the Bible to favor the subordination of women. They insist on literal interpretations of passages and language that reflect a cultural bias against women.

Biblical interpretation is called hermeneutics. Some people say that they do not interpret the Bible but just take it at face value; nonetheless, all reading of Scripture involves interpretation. We interpret when we select what to emphasize. We interpret when we apply the biblical message to ourselves. We interpret when we teach the biblical message to our children and others. Since all of us who take the Bible seriously do interpret the Bible, it is important for us to have guidelines for interpretation.

One does not have to be a biblical scholar to interpret the Bible according to these basic hermeneutical principles: (1) the grammatical principle; (2) the historical principle; (3) the contextual principle; (4) the theological principle.

The grammatical principle involves the study of the meaning of words and the relationship between words in the Bible. Even without knowledge of the original Hebrew and Greek languages of the Bible, a person can study the words in the Bible with the aid of Bible dictionaries, commentaries, and various translations. For example, a Bible dictionary or commentary will reveal the meaning of the word Jesus often used to address God. The word translated "Father" in the Lord's Prayer (Matt. 6:9) is the Aramaic word *Abba*, an intimate word small children used for their fathers. It is closer to the modern word "Daddy" than "Father." By using this word Jesus was teaching the accessible love and care of God, not a rigid view of God as masculine.

The word "Mother" today could express as well or better Jesus' teaching concerning intimate relationship with God.

The historical principle of biblical interpretation involves a study of the situation in which the Bible was originally written. Bible atlases, commentaries, and historical studies of biblical culture will aid us. When we understand the male-dominated culture in which the Bible was written, we can understand why the majority of the biblical language for God is masculine. The culture in which the Bible was written considered females as property of fathers and then husbands. One of the Ten Commandments includes a man's wife among his possessions, along with his house, slaves, and animals (Exod. 20:17). It is little wonder that a society which put such low value upon women would not refer to God as female. Seen in the light of this historical setting, the many feminine images of God in the Bible take on great significance.[9] The Living Word of God was miraculously breaking through historical and cultural limitations.

The contextual principle of biblical interpretation recognizes that every passage must be interpreted in light of other passages. We must interpret a passage in light of what immediately precedes and follows that passage, in light of the basic themes and literary form of the biblical book in which it comes, and in light of the overall message of the Bible. Down through the centuries biblical interpreters have taken the masculine language for God out of the context of the whole biblical revelation. They have so overemphasized the masculine God of the Bible that few laypeople have any knowledge of a God beyond the male gender. For example, in preaching and teaching Luke 15, most give far more emphasis to the parables of the lost sheep and the prodigal son, which picture God as a man, than to the parable of the lost coin, which pictures God as a woman. And they are quick to compare the man in the parable of the lost sheep to God, but rarely compare the woman in the parallel parable of the lost coin to God. They thus fail to interpret the parable of the lost coin in its proper context.

When we follow the theological principle of biblical interpretation, we study a passage in light of the major truths of the Bible. For the Christian, Jesus Christ is the ultimate Truth by which everything else in the Bible is to be interpreted. The unifying theme of the Bible is God's saving, liberating grace most fully revealed in Christ. Christ's resurrection brings hope of new life in our relationship with God and with people. Throughout biblical revelation we see God taking the side of the poor and liberating the oppressed. Jesus came to "preach good news to the poor... proclaim release to the captive... set at liberty those who are oppressed" (Luke 4:18). The truth of God's revelation in Christ sets us free (John 8:32). These basic theological truths lead us beyond a literalistic interpretation of the masculine references to God in the Bible. Rev. Patricia Gladney Holland tells of hearing her pastor include in his benediction the biblical image of God as a comforting mother (Isa. 66:13). She tells of the spiritual liberation she experienced: "I knew what it was like to be comforted by a mother. What was released was the barrier. The fact that what we feel is release indicates something was blocked — a barrier removed — a stone rolled away."[10]

As Christians we preach and teach a resurrection theology. A resurrection interpretation of the Bible follows. New life comes from rolling away the stone of our patriarchal interpretation of the Bible. Opening ourselves to a God beyond masculine experience brings new freedom in our relationships with God and with one another. The Good News of Christ continually renews our lives. In this way the written Word of God becomes the Living Word transforming our lives. No biblical interpretation is complete until it finds meaningful, practical application in our lives. When we sing the hymn "Break Thou the Bread of Life," we express this longing for the Bible to become God's living presence in our lives: "Beyond the sacred page I seek Thee, Lord; my spirit pants for Thee, O living Word." Interpreting the Bible in ways that unlimit God from the masculine gender will enable women and other oppressed groups to experience the living, liberating Word.

Some people say that they can call God "he" without meaning a literal masculine God. But although our minds may be able to think about a Spirit God beyond gender, our imaginations picture a male God when we hear God called only "he," "Father," and "King." For this reason people talk about God as "the man upstairs." Children and many adults, when asked how they imagine God, will describe a male being, often a grandfatherly figure. Our masculine language for God imprints indelible masculine images of God in our minds. Our language for God then becomes crucial to the way we experience God and communicate God.

An interpretation of the Bible in light of its basic theology of liberation and resurrection leads to change in our language for God. Changing the masculine references in the Bible is in keeping with changes in translation and interpretation down through the centuries for clearer, more meaningful communication of the Word of God. God's truth must speak forth clearly in today's world. Thus we need to change masculine language in the Bible and in all our worship liturgy to language inclusive of female and male. These changes may be inconvenient and uncomfortable for us. But following Christ has never been comfortable or convenient. Through moving beyond masculine language for God, we will be more consistent with our theology of God as transcendent Spirit. At the same time we will all experience liberation in our relationships with God and with one another.

Questions for Discussion

1. What is the difference between revelation and inspiration?

2. In what ways is God's revelation apparent today?

3. How does God's inspiration of the biblical writers differ from the inspiration of other great writers and composers?

4. Examine the words of the hymn "Break Thou the Bread of Life." Which theory of biblical inspiration discussed in this chapter is most consistent with the message of this hymn?

5. How would the Bible have been different if it had been written by women in a matriarchal (female-dominated) culture?

6. What ways of addressing God do you think show the greatest respect?

7. What names for God do you feel most comfortable with?

8. Why have people down through history resisted new translations of the Bible?

9. How would you feel about an inclusive language translation of the Bible that takes out the pronoun "he" for God

and repeats the word "God" or other non-masculine names for God?

10. What are the reasons given for inclusive language translations of the Bible today?

11. How has the Bible been used to oppose social reforms?

12. Explain the basic principles of biblical interpretation. How do they apply to the present-day discussion of inclusive language in the church?

Chapter 2

The Unlimited God of Scripture

As an eagle stirreth up her nest, fluttereth over her young, spreadeth abroad her wings, taketh them, beareth them on her wings: So the Lord alone did lead him, and there was no strange god with him" (Deut. 32:11–12, KJV).

O Jerusalem, Jerusalem . . . how often would I have gathered your children together as a hen gathers her brood under her wings, and you would not! (Matt. 23:37)

The Bible does not limit God to masculine images. God as Father is not the only image in Scripture. Faithfulness to the complete biblical revelation leads us to include other images.

Opening our minds to new ideas can be scary at first. Growing up I learned that God is Spirit, far greater than we can imagine. But I also learned to speak of God as "he," "Father," and "King." I could not picture a Spirit, so these words naturally led me to imagine God as a male human being. In my mind I pictured God as a kind, powerful, and strict male authority. Many years before I went to seminary, my concept of God matured and expanded. I still used masculine terms, however, to refer to God. While I was in seminary, God used a systematic theology class and a personal experience to help me understand the inadequacy of our masculine language for God.

I was exhausted. For almost two years I had been commuting one hundred miles to seminary and teaching a full load of college English, in addition to being a wife and mother. Balancing the demands of family, teaching, studying, and traveling made this the most demanding period of my life. Often I was so tired that I would have to fight desperately to keep from falling asleep at the wheel. One night I was singing and praying, trying to keep awake. When I tried to pray "Our Father," as was my custom, something within me balked. I felt a strong need to be nurtured as a mother nurtures her children. With fear and trembling I tried out the words, "Our Mother." Would I be struck dead? But instead of fear and guilt, I felt an overwhelming sense of peace and comfort. Something in me was released: an affirmation of myself and of God. I experienced a sense of being held, of being carried.

As I approached graduation from seminary, I realized that the least adequate male student had a better opportunity of pastoring a church than I did. I struggled with feelings of hurt and anger. Praying to God as Mother helped me feel that God was on my side and just as incensed over discrimination against women as I was. Using the feminine images of God in praying has also helped me put greater value on my mothering and on what my mother did for me. Her nurturing love taught me the availability of a God who hears the cries of people.

Although taking the risk of openness to new experiences with God can be scary, we will find the resulting growth in faith rewarding and exhilarating. The commandment against worshipping idols includes more than physical statues. We create an idol when we become set in the way we picture and speak about God. Anything that becomes carved in our minds as an unalterable concept of God is an idol. Although the Bible pictures God as Father, it gives us a wide variety of other pictures. If we insist on imagining and speaking of God only in masculine terms, we have created God in the image of a masculine human being and have thus broken the commandment against making graven images (Exod. 20:4). Reclaiming other biblical images of God opens our minds and hearts to the vast possibilities of God.

In the Beginning

The first chapter of Genesis provides the foundation for our understanding of God. Here we find God giving birth to the universe. The feminine metaphor of God in labor pervades the creation account. The Hebrew word *Elohim*, used for God here at the beginning of the Bible, includes the feminine. *Elohim*, which is plural in form, seems to be derived from an ancient Semitic female god, *Eloah*, and a male god, *El*. This mingling of feminine and masculine forms for God indicates both inclusiveness and transcendence of all sexuality.[1]

The Spirit of God moved over the face of the waters to bring forth light and life. In the second verse of Genesis, the Hebrew word for Spirit (*Ruach*) is feminine in form. The word translated "moved" (*rachaph*) also means "flutter over." Deut. 32:11 uses the same word to compare God to a mother eagle fluttering over her young. The Bible uses the word *rachaph* to describe God's action only in Genesis 1:2 and Deut. 32:11.

Thus we see that the first word for God in Scripture includes the feminine, the first word for Spirit is feminine, and the first picture of God is a mother eagle giving birth to the world. These feminine images for God, given prominence at the very beginning of the Bible, deserve our attention.

The writer of Genesis comes to the creation of humanity and describes God in dialogue. "Let us make humanity in our image, after our likeness; and let them have dominion over the fish of the sea, and over the birds of the air, and over the cattle, and over all the earth, and over every creeping thing that creeps upon the earth" (Gen. 1:26). Some theologians, reading a Christian viewpoint back into the Hebrew Bible, have seen here the first reference to the Trinity. Whether Christ and the Holy Spirit participated with God in creation is not the issue here. The point is that the writer of Genesis depicts God's diversity in unity. From the beginning God could not be captured in a single image. The divine "us" creates "them" in "our" likeness. And this likeness includes male and female. "So God created humanity in his own image, in the image of God he created him; male and female he created them" (Gen. 1:27). If male and female are in the image of God, then God's image includes male and female. Although the image of God implies much more than sexuality, this passage makes clear that femaleness and maleness are in some way part of God's nature.

This first chapter of Genesis clearly indicates the inadequacy of the words "he" and "him" for God. The creation account depicts God as including female and male, but then uses masculine terms to refer to God. This is not surprising given the limits of the Hebrew language and culture. Like English, Hebrew has no singular personal pronoun form that includes both male and female. In a patriarchal culture that did not even value a woman's testimony in a court of law, the only way to honor God was through the use of masculine words. What is amazing is the prominence given feminine images of God at the beginning of Scripture. Although human beings have attempted to capture God in masculine language, God continually escapes.

Genesis 1 presents God as Creator. God brought light out of darkness. God flung the sun and stars into the heavens. God filled the world with such a variety of plants and animals that scientists still have not classified all of them. The pinnacle of creation was male and female in the image of God. Humanity thus partakes of the creativity and the rationality of God and of the femaleness and maleness of God.

Those who take the first chapter of Genesis seriously must come to grips with the female, as well as the male, image of God. To imagine God and to refer to God as male only is to let the part stand for the whole. While all images of God are seeing "in part," groping to accommodate the infinite to human understanding, we come closer to the Whole by beginning where biblical revelation begins: with God as male and female.

Other Old Testament Pictures of God

In a key passage in Exodus, God renews the covenant with Israel. Even though the people had shown the worst kind of unfaithfulness in worshipping the Golden Calf, God offers another chance. The Hebrew word *rahum* conveys the continued graciousness, mercy, and compassion of God: "I will be gracious to whom I will be gracious, and will show mercy [*rahum*] on whom I will show mercy" (Exod. 33:19). The Hebrew word here rendered "mercy" can be translated "womb-love."[2] This passage suggests God as a Mother who continually loves and nurtures even wayward children.

The strong, tender maternal image recurs in the Song of Moses. Moses praises God for taking care of Israel in the wilderness: "As an eagle stirreth up her nest, fluttereth over her young, spreadeth abroad her wings, taketh them, beareth them on her wings: So the Lord alone did lead him, and there was no strange god with him" (Deut. 32:11–12, KJV). The mother eagle represents the nature of God in relationship to her children. The female eagle, larger and heavier than the male, bears the eaglets on her wings when it is time for them to leave the nest. The mother eagle stirs up her nest to get the young out on their own to hunt their own food. Then she takes them on her wings and swoops down suddenly to force them to fly alone. But she always stays close enough to swoop back under them when they become too weary and weak to continue to fly on their own.[3] Through this powerful image of God as a mother eagle, we can understand God as nurturing and supporting us when we are weak, yet always encouraging us to grow and mature. Like the mother eagle, God tenderly and lovingly guides her children toward maturity.

The prophet Hosea pictures God as a loving Mother who agonizes over her children's waywardness. God has patiently taught them to walk and tenderly taken them into her arms when they have fallen. "Yet it was I who taught Ephraim to walk, I took them up in my arms; but they did not know that I healed them" (Hos. 11:3). As a mother mourns a straying child, God laments: "How can I give you up, O Ephraim! How can I hand you over, O Israel!" (11:8)

Hosea later presents a less tender female image of God. Because the Israelites did not show faithfulness and gratitude to God for delivering them out of Egypt and for sustaining them in the wilderness, God is as furious as a bereaved mother bear. "I will fall upon them like a bear robbed of her cubs, I will tear open their breast" (Hos. 13:8).

The prophet Isaiah combines masculine and feminine images of God. In Isaiah 42:13, we see God marching forth "like a mighty man of war," and in verse 14 we hear God crying out "like a woman in travail." Here Isaiah gives us a balanced picture of God. The military figure presents God prevailing over his enemies. The poet then shifts from God as a warrior to God as a woman in childbirth. God in her pain over the unfaithfulness of her children, who have deserted her to follow graven images, cries out like a woman in labor. In describing the intensity of God's suffering love, Isaiah foreshadows Christ's suffering that makes possible the new birth.

Isaiah 63 again balances female and male attributes of God.

Look down from heaven and see, from thy holy and glorious habitation. Where are thy zeal and thy might? The yearning of thy heart and thy compassion are withheld from me. For thou art our Father, though Abraham does now know us and Israel does not acknowledge us; thou, O Lord, art our Father, our Redeemer from of old is thy name. (Isa. 63: 15–16)

The phrase here rendered "the yearning of thy heart" can be translated "the trembling of thy womb and thy compassion." The prophet longs for the maternal, womb-like compassion of God. Shifting from maternal to paternal language, the writer calls on the God of the womb to be a compassionate Father.[4] This mixture of maternal and paternal metaphors teaches us not to limit God to either male or female characteristics.

Another passage in Isaiah presents the curious image of a masculine God carrying children in his womb:

Hearken to me, O house of Jacob, all the remnant of the house of Israel, who have been borne by me from your birth, carried from the womb; even to your old age I am He; and to gray hairs I will carry you: I have made, and I will bear; I will carry, and will save. (Isa. 46:3–4)

In a male-dominated culture, Isaiah could use only the masculine pronoun to give God the proper respect. But it is clear that only the feminine description of God as tender Mother, bearing and delivering her children at birth and throughout life, could express the love God extends to her children. Here, as in other passages, the coming together of feminine and masculine images indicates that God includes and transcends male and female.

Isaiah assures the Israelites that God will not forsake them, depicting God as a nursing mother. The people feel that God has forsaken them. Isaiah comforts them by comparing God to a nursing mother who cannot forget her children whom she has tenderly suckled. "Can a woman forget her sucking child, that she should have no compassion on the son of her womb? Even these may forget, yet I will not forget you" (Isa. 49:15). This image illuminates the intimacy and constancy of God's relationship with her children. Nothing can sever the bond between the mother and the child whom she has carried in her womb and nursed at her breast. So it is with God and her children.

Isaiah again reassures Israel with the picture of a comforting Mother God: "As one whom his mother comforts, so I will comfort you; you shall be comforted in Jerusalem" (Isa. 66:13). Isaiah has been depicting Jerusalem as the mother who nurses and carries her children. Now the picture changes to God as the Mother to whom the children come for consolation. The exiled people could take heart in this promise that God would bring them once more to Jerusalem, tenderly and lovingly comforting them as a mother comforts her children. The *Interpreter's Bible* calls this picture of God as a comforting Mother "one of the Bible's most cherished expressions for God's grace."[5]

The psalmist pictures God as a protective and loving mother bird, providing refuge for humanity under her wings. "Be merciful unto me, O God ... for in thee my soul takes refuge; in the shadow of thy wings I will take refuge, till the storms of destruction pass by" (Ps. 57:1).[6] We can find warmth and protection under God's wings. The same God who as mother eagle pushes us out of the nest so that we can become independent is also the mother hen who provides security under her loving wings.[7]

The psalmist brings masculine and feminine images together to describe the relationship between humanity and God. "Behold, as the eyes of servants look unto the hand of their masters, as the eyes of a maid to the hand of her mistress, so our eyes look to the Lord our God, till [God] have mercy upon us" (Ps. 123:2). Here we see God compared to the head man and the head woman in the ancient household. As the male servants looked to their master and the female servants looked to their mistress for their orders and sustenance, so we look to God. Again the image of God as masculine alone will not suffice. A fuller picture of God is necessary to show more clearly who God is and to include all humanity in relationship to God.

In the psalms God acts in another intimate female role, that of midwife. "Yet thou art [God] who took me from the womb, thou didst keep me safe upon my mother's breasts. Upon thee was I cast from my birth, and since my mother bore me thou hast been my God" (Ps. 22:9-10). Feeling forsaken and persecuted, the poet finds reassurance in this picture of God's tender care beginning at birth. The image of God as midwife joins with the image of God as mother to strengthen the biblical picture of God's intimate involvement with us.[8]

One of the Hebrew names for God, *El Shaddai*, suggests a feminine picture of God. *El Shaddai*, usually translated "God Almighty," can also mean "God of the breasts," or "the Breasted God."[9] Genesis 49:25 contains a wordplay between the adjective translated "Almighty" (*Shaddai*) and the noun translated "breasts" (*shaddim*). Jacob tells his sons that the tribes of Joseph will receive blessings "by the God of your father who will help you, by God Almighty who will bless you with blessings of heaven above, blessings of the deep that couches beneath, blessings of the breasts and of the womb." This verse suggests God as Mother, giving the blessings of the breasts and the womb.[10] Biblical interpreters and translators have emphasized *El Shaddai* as a male God of war over *El Shaddai* as a female God with breasts. However, both interpretations are valid. Some biblical writers realized that God reflects the whole of humanity, not just the masculine. From its very beginning, monotheism has resisted an exclusively masculine God.[11]

Biblical revelation explicitly presents God as female in the wisdom literature. The book of Proverbs reveals divine Wisdom as feminine. The Hebrew word for "wisdom" (*hokmah*) is grammatically feminine, feminine pronouns are used to refer to "wisdom," and verb forms and adjectives used with this noun reflect the feminine gender.

> Wisdom cries aloud in the street; in the markets she raises her voice.... Give heed to my reproof; behold, I will pour out my thoughts to you; I will make my words known to you.... those who listen to me will dwell secure and will be at ease, without dread of evil. (Prov. 1:20, 23, 33)

Here Wisdom is clearly a feminine image of God, just as elsewhere fatherhood is a masculine image of God.[12]

Wisdom cherishes, exalts, and rewards those who are faithful to her:

> Get wisdom; get insight. Do not forsake her, and she will keep you; love her, and she will guard you.... Prize her highly, and she will exalt you; she will honor you if you

embrace her. She will place on your head a fair garland; she will bestow on you a beautiful crown. (Prov. 4:5b–6, 8–9)

In addition to masculine and feminine images to describe God, the Old Testament writers used many other word pictures. The Hebrews emphasized that their God was not an earthbound being, but the high and lofty God of the universe. This God could not be located in just one place nor described by one image alone. Thus the biblical writers use many analogies in their attempt to describe God. Nonhuman, along with human, metaphors help reveal a God beyond words.

One of the most common names for God in the Old Testament is "Holy One of Israel." The writer of Isaiah often uses this designation in parallel construction with *Yahweh*. "For I am the Lord [*Yahweh*] your God, the Holy One of Israel, your Savior" (Isa. 43:3). In Isaiah 17:7, "Holy One of Israel" is synonymous with "Maker." "In that day" people "will regard their Maker, and their eyes will look to the Holy One of Israel." Isaiah also links "Holy One of Israel" with "Redeemer": "I will help you, says the Lord; your Redeemer is the Holy One of Israel" (41:14b).[13]

In many passages the Bible calls God simply the "Holy One." "I am the Lord, your Holy One, the creator of Israel, your King" (Isa. 43:15).[14] The designation "Holy One" has special significance for this study. The meaning of the Hebrew word translated "holy" is that which is separate, cut off from all profane contact or use. The Hebrew writers make clear that God alone is holy. God transcends language and all other created reality. The word "holy" suggests that which is wholly Other, apart from all else. Perhaps this is the closest we can come to an accurate name for God. The writer of Isaiah suggests the inadequacy of all analogies: "To whom then will you compare me, that I should be like him? says the Holy One" (40:25). The psalmist condemns the Israelites for provoking and limiting "the Holy One of Israel" when they wandered in the wilderness: "they turned back and tempted God, and limited the Holy One of Israel" (Ps. 78:41, KJV). Any worship today that limits God to masculine language likewise comes under judgment.

The Psalms often employ "rock" as a metaphor for God. In

parallel construction with "fortress," it suggests strength. "Yea, thou art my rock and my fortress; for thy name's sake lead me and guide me" (Ps. 31:3). The "rock" image, linked with "refuge," suggests protection. "But the Lord has become my stronghold, and my God the rock of my refuge" (Ps. 94:22). The psalmist also joins "rock" with "salvation" to picture deliverance and victory. God "only is my rock and my salvation" (Ps. 62:2a). The idea of security and permanence also comes from the "rock" metaphor. "Trust in the Lord for ever, for the Lord God is an everlasting rock" (Isa. 26:4). These meanings come together in Psalm 18:2: "The Lord is my rock, and my fortress, and my deliverer, my God, my rock, in whom I take refuge, my shield, and the horn of my salvation, my stronghold."[15]

Another prominent nonhuman metaphor for God found throughout biblical revelation is light. God as light provides strength and clarity: "The Lord is my light and my salvation; whom shall I fear?" (Ps. 27:1) The image of God as light suggests total, permanent well-being. In a Messianic passage the prophet Isaiah employs this figure of speech: "The sun shall be no more your light by day, nor for brightness shall the moon give light to you by night; but the Lord will be your everlasting light, and your God will be your glory" (Isa. 60:19).[16]

The Hebrew Bible reveals a richness and diversity of word pictures for God. Focusing on the masculine images alone is like trying to define a tree by looking only at the leaves. The reality of the tree cannot be known without examining the roots and trunk and branches and fruit as well. Likewise we cannot experience God's reality by looking only at masculine images in Scripture. Biblical revelation offers so much more.

New Testament Images

God's revelation in the New Testament challenges us beyond masculine concepts of God. The New Testament reveals a God unlimited by masculine gender. Through figurative language and parables Jesus leads us toward fuller understanding and experience of God. Although the New Testament presents the image of God as Father, it offers a variety of other images.

Jesus' comparison of himself to a mother hen evidences his commitment to a portrayal of God who is more than masculine:

"O Jerusalem, Jerusalem, killing the prophets and stoning those who are sent to you! How often would I have gathered your children together as a hen gathers her brood under her wings, and you would not!" (Matt. 23:37).[17]

This poignant picture of God longing for her wayward children recalls Old Testament figures of God's tender, yearning mother love.[18] These words of Jesus also parallel the Old Testament mother bird images considered above. The Spirit of God who fluttered over the waters to bring forth creation is the same God who in Christ wants to re-create rebellious human creatures under her loving wings. Jesus longs to be the loving mother who gives her children the best gifts. This maternal image helps us to feel the unconditional love of Christ.

The mother bird images in Scripture and especially Jesus' comparison of himself to a mother hen contribute to Christian symbolism. In Christian art, one of the most widely used pictures of Christ's atonement is the Pelican-in-Her-Piety. This depiction of a pelican derives from the legend that in times of famine the female pelican tears open her breast and feeds her young with her own blood, dying that they may live. Another variation of this legend is that a serpent's sting kills the pelican's young. Mourning over her dead brood, the pelican plucks open her breast, and her blood flowing upon them restores their lives. In like manner, Christ's blood gives us restored life.[19]

In two parables Jesus further adds to our understanding of the depth of God's love and the inclusiveness of God's nature. In the parable of the lost sheep Jesus pictures God as a man, and in the parable of the lost coin Jesus pictures God as a woman (Luke 15:1–10). God is like a man who leaves ninety-nine sheep to go in search of one lost sheep. When he finds the sheep, he tenderly carries it back home and calls his friends and neighbors to rejoice with him. God is also like a woman who loses one of her coins. Because the lost coin is so precious to her, she searches diligently for it. When she finally finds the coin, she calls her friends and neighbors to share in her great joy.

These balanced images of God as male and female add to our understanding of the yearning, searching, inclusive love of God. In these parables Jesus presents main characters with whom both women and men can identify and at the same time pictures God whose image includes both male and female. The female and male images of God in these parables underscore Jesus' main point: God loves and places infinite value on each individual, female as well as male. The scribes and Pharisees who first heard these parables were probably shocked not only by God's total acceptance of immoral people, but also by Jesus' picturing God as female. If God could be female as well as male, then females might be worth as much as males. This was indeed a new revelation for a male-dominated society that did not value females enough even to allow them to hold property or to testify in a court of law.

In two other parables that balance female and male images of God, Jesus increases our understanding of the reign of God (Luke 13:18–21).[20] In the first Jesus pictures God as a man who plants a tiny mustard seed in his field. This smallest of seeds grows into a large tree. In the second parable Jesus shows God as a woman making bread. She mixes a tiny bit of yeast into a bushel of flour, and it grows and spreads throughout the whole mass. Again in twin parables Jesus chooses main characters who represent God as male and female. The main point of each parable is that out of the most minute, unlikely, insignificant, often invisible beginnings, God creates something extremely valuable. In God's hands the small becomes powerful. The representation of God as female as well as male illuminates this point. Jesus turns things upside down, challenging the attitudes and assumptions of disciples then and now. Though patriarchal society associates size and maleness with power, Jesus shows that the small and the female can also have tremendous power.

Jesus also challenges the assumptions of male-dominated culture through the image of God as Father. Some people have used Jesus' address of God as Father in his prayers as indisputable evidence that God is masculine. The prominent place of the Lord's Prayer in Christian tradition has reinforced this viewpoint. For many people, Jesus' teaching us to pray "Our Father who art in heaven" (Matt. 6:9) proves that God is a man. The word here translated "Father," however, is the Aramaic *Abba*, a babble-word which small children used for their fathers. This is an intimate way of addressing God, a word from the everyday speech of the family. The Jews of Jesus' day, trained to refrain from even speaking the name of God, were probably more shocked by such an intimate, non-traditional way of addressing God than some people are today when God is addressed as "Mother."

By calling God *Abba*, Jesus confronts the rigid, authoritarian role of the father in his male-dominated culture. Jesus calls us to a relationship that takes precedence over any natural family allegiance. "The one who loves father or mother more than me is not worthy of me; and the one who loves son or daughter more than me is not worthy of me" (Matt. 10:37). Jesus offers relationship within a new family joined by faith in God freely given. In addressing God as *Abba*, Jesus suggests a relationship of deepest intimacy and of individual freedom, as opposed to relationships in patriarchal society based on absolute obedience and necessity. Jesus' use of the word "Father," or *Abba*, for God includes something of what the word "mother" means.[21]

In using the "father" symbol for God, Jesus was not establishing the sex of the Godhead, nor was Jesus supporting the prevailing hierarchy in the families of the patriarchal society in which he lived. On the contrary, Jesus used this "father" symbol in such a way as to free people from the clutches of male domination. "That it has been interpreted out of context to present a male god who secures the primacy of the male is a situation that might be corrected by putting it back in context."[22] Jesus' references to God as Father were to stress the closeness of the divine-human bond, not to imply that the Creator of male and female was masculine.

Jesus' relationship to women, as well as to God, gives clear evidence that he radically opposed the norms of male-dominated society. In patriarchal society, women play no part in public life. But Jesus had women disciples:

Soon afterward Jesus went on through cities and villages, preaching and bringing the good news of the kingdom of God. And the twelve were with him, and also some women who had been healed of evil spirits and infirmities: Mary, called Magdalene, from whom seven demons had gone out, and Joanna, the wife of Chuza, Herod's steward, and Susanna, and many others, who provided for them out of their means. (Luke 8:1–3)[23]

These women left home and family and traveled openly with Jesus, a flagrant breach of custom. In Jewish society at this time, only males received instruction in the Torah, but Jesus spent time teaching women (Luke 10:38–41).[24] In patriarchal society, women could not serve as witnesses in court, but Jesus trusted women to be the first witnesses to the resurrection (Matt. 28:1–8).[25] Jesus treated women as full persons created in the image of God, who includes and transcends female and male.

One of the oldest texts of the New Testament records Jesus' calling the Holy Spirit "She." In the oldest Syriac version of the Bible, we find Jesus comforting the disciples before his crucifixion with these words: "The Spirit, the Paraclete, She shall teach you everything" (John 14:26). The Syriac word here translated "Spirit" is feminine in gender. Ancient Syriac writings, before the influence of Greek theology, always referred to the Holy Spirit as feminine. Later translators of the fifth century Syriac version, *Peshitta*, revealed their masculine bias by changing "She" to "He."[26]

Although most biblical translators and interpreters have referred to the Holy Spirit as "he," the original languages of the Bible do not support this masculine reference. Beginning with the first chapter of Genesis, and throughout the Hebrew Bible, the word for "Spirit" (*Ruach*) of God is feminine in gender. The Greek word used in the New Testament for "Spirit" (*Pneuma*) is neuter.

In attempting to personalize the Holy Spirit, translators of the New Testament have not been faithful to the original Greek. Since the Greek word for "spirit" is neuter, the most accurate English pronoun in reference to the Spirit would be "it." But this neuter pronoun is theologically and emotionally unsatisfactory. The Christian God is a personal God. The problem in English, as in Greek, is that there is no personal genderless singular pronoun. Translators have chosen the masculine personal pronoun. More faithful to total biblical revelation would be references to the Holy Spirit as "she." Such references present theological problems because the Holy Spirit transcends gender, but references to the Holy Spirit as "he" present the same problems. Until an inclusive singular personal pronoun becomes standard usage in English, the feminine personal pronoun is the more accurate.

The many references to the new birth in the New Testament also support our speaking of the Holy Spirit in feminine terms. In a passage that has become central to the Christian doctrine of salvation, Jesus says that we must be born of water and of the Spirit to have eternal life. "That which is born of the flesh is flesh, and that which is born of the Spirit is spirit" (John 3:6).[27] The Spirit performs the female function of giving birth. The Hebrew Bible's images of God as a woman in labor reach their culmination in the New Testament picture of the Spirit giving new birth through the suffering love of Christ. The image of God as a Mother bringing forth life serves as a unifying strand throughout biblical revelation. In the first chapter of Genesis, we see the Spirit of God hovering over the waters and giving birth to all creation. After humanity breaks the old covenant, the Spirit of God incarnate in Christ gives birth to new creatures reconciled to God and fashioned for eternal life (2 Cor. 5:17–19). The picture of God as Mother giving birth links creation and redemption. This image is thus central to biblical revelation.

Jesus also refers to God as female Wisdom: "the Wisdom of God said, 'I will send them prophets and apostles, some of whom they will kill and persecute'" (Luke 11:49). The Greek word *Sophia*, here translated "Wisdom," is feminine. As we have seen, some passages of the Hebrew Bible present Wisdom as a symbol for God.

New Testament writers associate Wisdom with Christ. The apostle Paul refers to Christ as God's Wisdom: "we preach Christ crucified, a stumbling block to Jews and folly to Gentiles, but to those who are called, both Jews and Greeks, Christ the power of God and the wisdom of God" (1 Cor. 1:23–24).[28] The Gospel of John reveals Christ as "the way, and the truth, and the life" (John 14:6). Proverbs depicts Wisdom in parallel terms as the path, the knowledge, the way that ensures life (Prov. 4:11, 22, 26).

The personification of Wisdom in Proverbs 8 contributes to the connection between feminine Wisdom and Christ. Wisdom existed before creation, was the first created being, and was active in creation (Prov. 8:22–31). Likewise Jesus Christ was "before all things," the "first-born of all creation," and the creator of all things: "all things were created through [Christ] and for [Christ]" (Col. 1:15-17). Thus biblical revelation links the Hebrew concept of Lady Wisdom and Christ.

The symbol of Christ as the *Logos*, or Word of God, parallels the symbol of Christ as Wisdom. The first chapter of John, like the first chapter of Colossians, presents Christ with God in the beginning and actively involved in creation: "In the beginning was the Word, and the Word was with God, and the Word was God... all things were made through [the Word]" (John 1:1, 3). Richardson calls Paul's chapter on Christ as Wisdom and John's chapter on Christ as *Logos* "the highest peaks of Christological speculation in the New Testament."[29] The Creator and the Redeemer of the world are one. Masculine *Logos* and feminine Wisdom also converge in these pivotal passages. The New Testament pictures Christ as including the Greek concept of *Logos*, the rational principle that sustains the universe, and the Hebrew concept of divine Wisdom.

The Gospels of Matthew and Luke reveal Jesus identifying with Wisdom. Chiding the Pharisees for their failure to recognize the prophetic voice, Jesus concludes, "The Son of man has come eating and drinking, and you say, 'Behold a glutton and a drunkard, a friend of tax collectors and sinners!' Yet wisdom is justified by all her children" (Luke 7:34-35). This identification of Christ with feminine Wisdom reveals that the Incarnation uniquely combined male and female, as well as humanity and deity, time and eternity.

The Incarnation includes and expands upon the Hebrew Bible's metaphor of God as light. Jesus declares oneness with the God who is the psalmist's "light and salvation" (Ps. 27:1) by declaring, "I am the light of the world" (John 8:12).[30] Using the light image, the Apostle Paul connects God's first act of creation as recorded in Genesis with God's revelation in Christ. "For it is the God who said, 'Let light shine out of darkness,' who has shone in our hearts to give the light of the knowledge of the glory of God in the face of Christ" (2 Cor. 4:6). The Prologue to John's Gospel gives fullest expression to the description of Christ as light. Christ is the light of all people, the light that the darkness cannot overcome, the true light that enlightens everyone (John 1:4-5, 9). This metaphor implies the moral and religious perfection of Christ, and much more. The image of Christ as light points beyond human concepts and language. Heavenly visions of God and Christ thus employ light imagery. The holy city of the new heaven and new earth "has no need of sun or moon to shine upon it, for the glory of God is its light, and its lamp is the Lamb. By its light shall the nations walk" (Rev. 21:23–24a).

The New Testament pictures Christ as the "door" to eternal life. Jesus said, "I am the door;" all who enter by me "will be saved, and will go in and out and find pasture" (John 10:9). This figurative statement reinforces Christ's claim to be "the way, the truth, and the life" (John 14:6). The depiction of Jesus as the "door" to abundant, eternal life suggests the uniqueness of Christ.

The New Testament also pictures Christ as the "bread of life" (John 6:35, 48, 51). The spiritual food Christ offers can do much more than the manna that God gave the Israelites in the wilderness. The manna sustained life only temporarily, while the bread Christ offers brings eternal life. The image of Christ as "bread" reveals that Christ parallels but exceeds God's great miracles under the old covenant. The picture of Christ as "bread" provides the basis for one of the most important Christian rituals, the Lord's Supper. The figure of the "living bread" becomes the "flesh" of Christ that gives eternal life (John 6:51–57). This metaphor has defied logical explanations down through the centuries, giving rise to different interpretations of the communion ritual. Again figurative language suggests but cannot contain the essence of God in Christ.

The New Testament offers a wealth of images of God. God is not only like a forgiving father, but also like a mother hen longing for her straying offspring and a woman searching until she finds one lost coin. God in Christ is Lady Wisdom, divine Word, the Light of the world, the Door to eternal life, the Bread of life. Just as we cannot capture God in one Person, even so we cannot capture God in one image. To think and speak of God in masculine images alone is unbiblical and idolatrous. The diversity of biblical metaphors points to God not made by human hands or minds.

Questions for Discussion

1. How do you picture God?

2. What new ways of picturing God have you learned from this chapter?

3. How does the first chapter of Genesis reveal that God transcends gender?

4. How do you feel about the feminine images of God in the Bible?

5. Why do the biblical writers refer to God as "he"?

6. How do the biblical comparisons of God to a mother make you feel?

7. How would you feel if you called God "Mother" as well as "Father"?

8. What are two possible translations of the Hebrew name for God *El Shaddai*? Why do you think most biblical translators have avoided the feminine translation of this name?

9. How does the image of God as female Wisdom link the Hebrew Bible and the New Testament?

10. Which nonhuman images of God and Christ are most meaningful to you?

11. How does Christ reveal that God includes and transcends male and female?

12. Why don't we call the Holy Spirit "it"? How would you feel if you called the Holy Spirit "she"?

Chapter 3

How We Got Where We Are

But you also, Jesus, good Lord, are you not also Mother?
Are you not Mother, who are as a hen who gathers her own
chicks under her wings? Truly, Lord, you also are Mother.
For that which others have been in labor with and have born,
they have received from you.

(Anselm, eleventh century)

There is but one only living and true God, who is infinite in
being and perfection, a most pure spirit, invisible, without
body, parts, or passions, immutable, immense, eternal, in-
comprehensible, almighty, most wise, most holy, most free,
most absolute.

(Westminster Confession of Faith, seventeenth century)

The nurse who attended the birth of my first child had much to
learn about bedside manner. For almost two days I had been in
labor. The last six hours were especially painful and exhausting.
We rushed to the hospital at 2:00 a.m. After I had suffered hard
labor for several hours without any pain medication, the nurse
saw me clenching my fists and gritting my teeth to keep from
crying out. She said unsympathetically, "It's going to get much
worse. It's going to get much worse." She was right. The labor
did get much more painful before the blessed experience of birth.

Today Christians labor to give birth to a new kind of church.
This new church will affirm and nurture the gifts of all members.
Women and men will experience freedom to become all God
created us to be. This church will include female and male in

the language and leadership. Seeing God as including male and female, this church will become an instrument of healing and transformation in society.

Before this birth can take place, we have to understand the barriers of tradition that stand in our way. Male-female relationships in the church got much worse before they began to improve. In the first century the Apostle Paul wrote: "There is neither Jew nor Greek, there is neither slave nor free, there is neither male nor female; for you are all one in Christ Jesus" (Gal. 3:28). The first-century church gave women greater freedom and opportunity than they experienced anywhere else in the society of that time. The church today, however, is only beginning to realize the full implications of being "neither male nor female...in Christ Jesus." For centuries before the new birth we are experiencing today, things got much worse for women, and for men, in the church.

In the second century, Tertullian called women "the devil's gateway." In the third century, Origen taught that man is more like God than woman because he is more spiritual, that woman is fleshly and thus antithetical to the divine. In the fourth century, Augustine denied that women are made in the image of God. In the thirteenth century, Aquinas declared that women are "misbegotten males" formed from "some unsuitability of the material."

To solidify their power in the church, male leaders took the masculine bias of the Bible and carried it to the extreme. The resistance we feel to changing the masculine language of the church comes more from these traditions of negative attitudes toward women than from the Bible. As we have seen, the Bible gives sufficient support for including the feminine in our language for God and for people. Surveying some prominent theologians in Christian history can help us understand the mixed feelings we have today about changing the way we think and speak about God.

Even the most glaring misogynists (woman haters) had mixed feelings about the gender of God. Their reading of the Bible, along with their personal experience, kept them from totally denying the feminine characteristics of God. In their writings we find the biblical pictures of the womb of God the Father and of a feminine Holy Spirit. We even find explicit references to

Jesus as Mother. No matter how stifling the patriarchal atmosphere, the feminine aspect of God kept emerging as a reminder that God is indeed Spirit, far above the limitations of sexuality. Looking at how we got to where we are today in Christian history will help us labor toward the birth of a church in which male and female are truly one in Christ Jesus.

The Early Church

In his *Apology*, Justin Martyr (c.100–c.167) provides one of the earliest Christian statements about the nature of God. Charged with atheism and martyred for his non-conformity to the polytheism prevalent in the Roman society of his day, Justin defends Christians as worshipers of the true God. Justin states that this God, unlike idols, is not the work of human hands and thus not subject to human error. To attempt to construct material images of God, that is, "to transfer His incommunicable Name upon such corruptible and helpless things as wood and stone," is "the highest flight of human folly" and "the most injurious affront to the true God, Who is a God of glory and form ineffable."[1] Justin here attempts to describe a God far above images created by human beings. However, Justin seems unaware that his masculine references to God impose a human image upon God.

Like Justin, Clement of Alexandria (c. 150–c. 215) labored to establish Christianity in a pagan society. This early church father, among the first of the orthodox Christian writers, uses images of God as both Father and Mother. In describing the tender, nurturing love of God, Clement writes of "the milk of the Father, by which alone we infants are nourished." Christ, the Word of God, especially serves as "the care-soothing breast of the Father." In spite of a patriarchal culture that kept Clement from calling God "Mother," he could find no more appropriate image to describe the nurturing love of God than that of a nursing mother. Clement understands, however, that neither feminine nor masculine imagery alone can describe Christ's love for humanity: "The Word is all to the child, both father and mother, and tutor and nurse."[2]

Another influential early contributor to Christian doctrine was Origen (c. 185–c. 253), who attempted to demonstrate his enthusiasm for the Christian faith by becoming a martyr. After his mother prevented his martyrdom, he settled down to write over six thousand volumes on the Christian faith. Origen took the Bible literally, applying it to his own lifestyle. Following Jesus' words in Matthew 19:12, he refrained from marrying. When he faced sexual temptation, he took Matthew 5:30 literally and made himself a eunuch. His personal sexual struggles resulted in a negative attitude toward women. Origen taught that women are more closely connected to the flesh than men and thus not as spiritual. Origen could not, however, deny the feminine component in the Godhead. He equates female Wisdom with Christ, stating that "Wisdom" is the most ancient and most appropriate title given to Jesus. We experience Christ according to the way we embrace Wisdom, "in that He is wisdom." Origen follows the biblical use of female pronouns to refer to Wisdom: "see how well the Wisdom of God which is above every creature speaks of herself, when she says: 'God created me the beginning of His ways, for His works.' "[3]

Likewise, St. Ambrose (339–397), bishop of Milan, mixes male and female imagery in his description of God. Ambrose not only pictures the church as Mother, but also God as Mother. Refuting the Arian heresy, Ambrose mixes maternal and paternal images to emphasize that Jesus is of the same nature and substance as God: "Let us beware lest we separate the substance of the hidden nature of the only begotten Son from the bosom of the Father, and from, as it were, His paternal womb."[4] Though the image of the Father's womb appears strange to modern readers, it dramatically reveals that one of the most important early teachers of the Christian faith could not describe the nature of God with masculine images alone.

The most influential theologian of the early church was St. Augustine (354–430). Before his conversion to Christianity, Augustine adopted the dualistic Manichean philosophy, which stressed the essential evil of matter. This philosophy, along with his intense personal struggles with his own sexuality, resulted in his low opinion of women. Augustine associates women with the evil flesh that must be controlled by the spirit, which he believed was superior in men. In contradiction to Genesis 1:27, Augustine denies that woman is made in the image of God. Augustine goes to great lengths to refute an opinion of his day that the Holy Spirit is female, "the mother of the Son of God, and the wife of the Father; since...these things offend us in carnal things, because we think of bodily conceptions and births."[5] Thus it seems that Augustine's main objection to the image of the Holy Spirit as female is his repulsion to suggestions of sexuality in God. In referring to God as masculine only, Augustine somehow believes that he lifts God above sexuality.

In spite of the dualism and misogynism in his philosophy, Augustine cannot completely deny the female element in the divine. He links female Wisdom with Christ. Although he worries that thinking of wisdom as a woman might put sexual thoughts into a man's mind, Augustine nevertheless allows that Wisdom is a "woman in sex, since it is expressed in both Greek and Latin tongues by a word of the feminine gender."[6] In commenting upon the biblical image of Jesus as mother hen, Augustine equates Christ and feminine Divine Wisdom: "Let us put our egg under the wings of that Hen of the Gospel....For that hen is Divine Wisdom; but It assumed flesh to accommodate Itself to its chickens."[7] Although Augustine explicitly states that Wisdom is feminine in gender, here he uses the neuter pronoun to refer to Divine Wisdom. He thus will not consciously acknowledge the logical conclusion to his argument: that since Wisdom is feminine in gender, since Wisdom and Christ are one, and since Christ and God are one, then there is a female component in the Godhead.

Augustine admits his own limitations in thinking about God. To Augustine God is incomprehensible. The further Augustine goes in trying to comprehend the incomprehensible, the more expansive his description becomes. Over and over Augustine emphasizes that God is not a body, but an eternal, powerful, righteous, beautiful, blessed, unchangeable, wise Spirit. Even one of the most male-biased theologians in the early church cannot contain God in masculine images.

We can see that the founders of the early church included both masculine and feminine images to describe a God beyond human understanding. The feminine images are indeed significant because these early theologians labored under the prejudices of their male-dominated religion and society. In miraculous, mysterious ways God was slowly breaking free from patriarchy.

The Middle Ages

When we look at some of the Christian writings from the Middle Ages, we see an increase in maternal imagery for God. In the medieval devotional literature we find a growing tendency to emphasize the approachability of God. The maternal imagery helped to foster the ideas of the accessibility and tenderness of God and of our union with God.[8]

St. Anselm of Canterbury (1033–1109) stresses that God is not a body, but a supreme Spirit. Since God is not corporeal, Anselm believes that there is no distinction of sex in God or Christ. And he concedes that since the Bible refers to God and Christ as Truth and Wisdom, both feminine nouns, we could call them Mother and Daughter. He thinks, however, that it is more appropriate to refer to them as Father and Son because it is "a natural fact in most instances," that the male is the superior sex.[9] Thus Anselm's preference for male terminology for God is based more on cultural prejudice than on biblical revelation. In his own personal devotional life, however, Anselm transcends cultural prejudices and prays to Jesus as Mother, using the imagery of Matthew 23:37:

> But you also, Jesus, good Lord, are you not also Mother? Or are you not Mother, who are as a hen who gathers her own chicks under her wings? Truly, Lord, you also are Mother. For that which others have been in labor with and have born, they have received from you. You first on account of them have both died by being in travail with those whom they have given birth to, and have given birth to them by dying. For unless you had been in travail, you would not have died; and unless you had died, you would not have given birth.... You also, soul, dead by your own doing, run under the wings of Jesus your Mother, and complain of your pains under her wings. Demand that she tend your blows, and that life return to those fostered. Christ Mother, who gather your chicks under your wings, this your dead chick throws itself under your wings. For by your gentleness the terrified are comforted, by your perfume, the despairing are restored. Your warmth brings back to life the dead, your touch justifies sinners. Acknowledge, Mother, your dead

son, either through the sign of your cross, or through the voice of your confession.[10]

In his suffering, Anselm finds comfort in this picture of Jesus as a Mother giving birth and even dying to give her children life.

The French monastic reformer Bernard of Clairvaux (1090–1153) likewise uses maternal imagery to describe Jesus. In a sermon on the Song of Songs Bernard speaks of "the nurturing sweetness" of the breasts of Christ, the Bridegroom.[11] Bernard advises Hugh, a young novice, to draw nourishment and strength to endure the austerity of the monastic life from Christ, his Mother:

> The sweetness of Christ will take the bitterness from the prophet's broth. If you feel the stings of temptation, lift your eyes to the serpent on the staff, and draw life from the wounds of Christ. He will be your mother, and you will be his son. The nails which cleave his hands and feet, must also pass through yours.[12]

St. Bonaventure (1221–1274) likewise uses feminine pictures of Christ. Bonaventure, acknowledged as one of the greatest minds of the Christian Middle Ages by being declared a Doctor of the Church, describes the nourishing milk of Christ. Bonaventure says that for the strong believers the blood of Jesus is like wine, "but be you feeble, and a suckling still, it is for you sustaining milk."[13] Bonaventure also refers to Jesus as "God's Wisdom," which, as we have seen, is biblically and traditionally a feminine image. However, when Bonaventure attempts to contemplate the invisible essence of God, he drops gender-specific images and refers to God simply as "Being." As Bonaventure progresses in his understanding of God, he discovers that human images cannot describe God, who is "pure being, unqualified being, and absolute being."[14]

St. Thomas Aquinas (1225–1274), the most prolific and influential medieval theologian, likewise affirms that human descriptions of God are inadequate. In his most famous work, *Summa Theologiae*, Aquinas says that it is impossible to see the essence of God through any kind of created likeness. God is "beyond naming because his essence is beyond what we understand of him and the meaning of the names we use."[15] Aquinas does not seem to realize that his use of masculine pronouns suggests a created likeness of God. However, we can easily see why Aquinas chooses masculine instead of feminine words to refer to God. Aquinas says that the female is defective: "For the active power in the seed of the male tends to produce something like itself, perfect in masculinity; but the procreation of a female" results from some "debility of the active power" or "some unsuitability of the material."[16]

In spite of his misogynism, Aquinas cannot totally deny the feminine aspect of God. Like Origen and Augustine, Aquinas accepts the biblical connection between feminine Wisdom and Christ. Aquinas links the biblical mother hen image of Christ with Wisdom. He even refers to Christ as "our Mother, Wisdom of God."[17]

The fourteenth-century mystic Julian of Norwich (1342–c. 1413) developed fully the image of a Christian feminine divinity. When she was thirty years old, Dame Julian, living as a recluse in a cell attached to the Church of St. Julian at Norwich, received sixteen "shewings," or revelations, from God. In her vision of the Trinity, Julian saw three properties: Fatherhood, Motherhood, and Lordhood. "God, Almighty, is our kindly Father; and God, All-Wisdom, is our kindly Mother; with the Love and the Goodness of the Holy Ghost: which is all one God, one Lord."[18] Julian explains her vision of the all-inclusiveness of God while maintaining the unity of the Godhead:

As verily as God is our Father, so verily God is our Mother; and that shewed he in all, and especially in these sweet words where he saith: "I it am . . . the Might and the Goodness of the Fatherhood; I it am, the Wisdom of the Motherhood; I it am, the Light and the Grace that is all blessed Love: I it am, the Trinity, I it am, the Unity: I am the sovereign Goodness of all manner of things. I am that maketh thee to love: I am that maketh thee to long: I it am, the endless fulfilling of all true desires."[19]

The shift from the masculine to the neuter pronoun here indicates Julian's struggle to express a God beyond the limitations of gender.

But her visions reveal to her a God who has characteristics of a Mother as well as a Father. Julian sees the Motherhood of God as threefold: Creator, Sustainer, and Teacher. God gives birth to our flesh, and through Christ's passion and death gives birth to our spirits. Then "our precious Mother, Jesus," feeds us not with milk, but "with the Blessed Sacrament that is precious food of very life; and with all the sweet Sacraments he sustaineth us full mercifully and graciously." As a mother in teaching her children sometimes allows them to fall, so God may allow us to fall. However, "our heavenly Mother, Jesus, may not suffer us that are his children to perish." Our Gracious Mother raises us when we fall and "feedeth us and furthereth us: right as that high sovereign Kindness of Motherhood, and as kindly need of Childhood asketh."[20]

In the ongoing work toward a Christian doctrine of God, medieval writers used maternal images to reveal the accessibility of God in Christ. The image of God as female helped Julian and other medieval Christian writers to describe the tender, nurturing qualities of God. The mystical mind and spirit of the Middle Ages saw the feminine possibilities in God. These medieval writers we have surveyed also make clear that God far exceeds our capacity to conceive or name.

The Reformation

One of the Roman Catholic doctrines that the reformers protested was the divinity of Mary. Placing Scripture, instead of the papacy, at the center of authority, they viewed the church's veneration of Mary and the saints as unbiblical. This reaction against the tradition of Mary worship led many reformers to avoid any feminine images of God. God, however, continued to break through masculine images.

The Protestant Reformation began with Luther's ninety-five theses against ecclesiastical indulgences. Martin Luther (1483–1546) never intended to found a new church, but rather to work for reformation within the church. Luther agrees with Augustine that God is far greater than the human mind can conceive. There is no way that we can comprehend what God was doing before the creation. Now God is manifested only "through His works and the Word, because the meaning of these is understood in some measure."[21] Though Luther takes the masculine pronouns of the Bible literally, he also understands through the Word the image of a feminine Holy Spirit giving birth to the universe:

> As a hen broods her eggs, keeping them warm in order to hatch her chicks, and as it were, to bring them to life through heat, so Scripture says that the Holy Spirit brooded, as it were, on the waters to bring to life those substances which were to be quickened and adorned. For it is the office of the Holy Spirit to make alive.[22]

Luther takes seriously other biblical images of feminine divinity. Commenting on Isaiah 46:3, Luther says that God could not "speak more sweetly than in transferring a mother's experiences to Himself.... God cares for us with an everlasting maternal heart and feeling." With a heart full of concern, God says to us, "Come to Me, I will carry you in My womb." Luther interprets the womb of God to be the divine Word, or Scripture, and he exhorts us to "cling to the Word alone, and we shall have God as a mother who feeds us and carries us and frees us from all evils." Likewise Luther finds great comfort in the maternal image of God in Isaiah 49:15. Luther says that the writer of Isaiah employs the figure of a woman to reveal the depth of God's love for her children. God says to us, "I will not forsake you, because I am your mother. I cannot desert you." In commenting on Isaiah 66:13, Luther says that when we suffer, God comforts us as a mother hugs and comforts a child at her breast. Through faith and the Word we receive a "profoundly paternal love and thoroughly maternal caresses."[23] Thus Luther helps us to feel both the motherly and fatherly love of God for us.

More radical than Luther in abolishing Roman Catholic traditions of worship, Ulrich Zwingli (1484–1531) led the reform in Zurich, Switzerland. Zwingli opposed the worship of Mary because she is a created being, not Deity. Zwingli's strong reaction against the veneration of any created being resulted in little male or female imagery in his doctrinal statements on God. Zwingli states that the "one and only uncreated thing is God, for there can be but one uncreated thing."[24] In the account of his faith submitted to the Roman Emperor, Zwingli states that "God is one and He alone is God, and that He is by nature good, true, powerful, just, wise, the Creator and Preserver of all things visible and invisible; that Father, Son and Holy Spirit are indeed three persons, but that their essence is one and single."[25] A product of his patriarchal culture, Zwingli overlooks the fact that his masculine references to God suggest a created being. Zwingli and other theologians we have considered betray their bias when they use masculine pronouns to refer to that Being beyond all human beings.

A prominent figure in the radical Reformation was the Dutch Menno Simons (c. 1496–1561). His followers, who came to be known as Mennonites, were radical in their elimination of all traditions in favor of biblical authority. Menno Simons declares that God is the only "eternal, living, Almighty sovereign God and Lord...and since He is a Spirit so great, terrible, and invisible, He is also ineffable, incomprehensible, and indescribable, as may be deduced and understood from the Scriptures." Although Menno Simons draws masculine references to God from the Scriptures, he also employs the biblical image of God as feminine Wisdom. From the New Testament he takes the equation of Christ and personified Wisdom. Jesus Christ is "the first and only begotten Son, the first-born of every creature, the eternal Wisdom, the power of God, the everlasting Light, the eternal Truth, the everlasting Life, the eternal Word."[26] True to biblical revelation, Menno Simons does not limit God or Christ to a single masculine or feminine image. Instead he helps us to expand our concept of God through many biblical metaphors.

In Geneva, John Calvin (1509–1564) developed a form of Protestantism that spread to France, Holland, Scotland, Poland, and Hungary. Like other reformers, Calvin placed the Bible at the center of religious authority. Calvin believed that although God is manifested in the universe and in all creatures, Scripture provides the main source of our knowledge about God. The Bible prohibits us from giving any visible form to God. "God's glory is corrupted by an impious falsehood whenever any form is attached to him." The commandment against making a graven image "restrains our waywardness from trying to represent him by any visible image."[27] Calvin seems totally unaware that the masculine pronoun attaches a form to God and creates a visible form in the minds of people.

Calvin does, however, provide some balance in his commentary on the feminine imagery for God in the book of Isaiah. In Scripture Calvin finds powerful metaphors comparing God to a mother. The picture of God crying out like a woman in labor (Isa. 42:14) "expresses astonishing warmth of love and tenderness of affection." God "compares himself to a mother who singularly loves her child, though she brought him forth with extreme pain." In answer to those critics who might say that this maternal image is not applicable to God or is degrading to the majesty and power of God, Calvin says that "in no other way than by such figures of speech can his ardent love towards us be expressed." Isaiah also helps us understand the depth of God's love for us through the comparison of God to a mother carrying a child in her womb (Isa. 46:3). To the objection "that God is everywhere called 'a Father,' and that this title is more appropriate to him," Calvin replies "that no figures of speech can describe God's extraordinary affection towards us." Calvin believes, however, that the maternal images in the Bible help express this incomparable love of God. Calvin states that the intention of the prophet Isaiah is to show the Jews "that they were not begotten in vain, and that God, who has manifested himself to be both their Father and their Mother, will always assist them."[28] Calvin elaborates on other biblical images of God as Mother, stating that God was not satisfied "with proposing the example of a father...but in order to express his very strong affection, he chose to liken himself to a mother."[29]

Calvin and other reformers struggled to describe a God beyond description and to express the inexpressible love of God. Although we do not find the extensive maternal imagery in Reformation theology that we find in medieval Christian writers, the reformers' emphasis on the centrality of Scripture led them to recognize the importance of the biblical feminine images of God. They discovered in the biblical materials a God who includes female and male and much more. Those of us today who place priority on Scripture as God's revelation can follow the example of the reformers in expanding concepts of God to include the feminine. It is our responsibility to continue their work toward a doctrine of God. We can take the comments of these earlier theologians to their logical conclusion and eliminate mas-

culine pronouns to refer to God. In this way our language will
be more consistent with our belief in a God beyond all human
forms.

The Modern Church

The nineteenth and twentieth centuries have brought changes in
theology, but little change in the masculine language used to refer to God. Theologians have continued to affirm, ever more
emphatically, the transcendence and unknowableness of God
and the inadequacy of all human thoughts about God. Modern
theologians have thus used less human imagery for God than
theologians in previous eras. They have, however, tenaciously
held to traditional masculine references to God. Even those who
have questioned the authority of tradition and Scripture have
continued to refer to God as "he." We have a tendency to cling
to our habitual language for God, whether or not we agree with
its implications. Nevertheless, as in previous centuries, a more
inclusive God keeps emerging.

Friedrich Schleiermacher (1768–1834), acknowledged as the
father of modern theology, placed religious experience as pre-
eminent in leading human beings to God. The authority of
Scripture and tradition were secondary. Schleiermacher sought
to eliminate all human analogies from his doctrine of God. He
elaborates upon attributes of God, such as omnipotence and in-
finity, rather than analogies for God. Schleiermacher opposes
the comparison of any of the attributes of God with human
characteristics.[30] Schleiermacher, for the most part, steers clear
of analogies for God, rarely even using the analogy of God as Father. However, his exclusive use of masculine pronouns to refer
to God naturally leads us to compare God's attributes to those
of male human beings.

The Danish philosopher and theologian Søren Kierkegaard
(1813–1855) interpreted the Christian faith in light of existen-
tial philosophy. Like Schleiermacher, Kierkegaard believed that
our knowledge of God comes through experience rather than rational proofs. Kierkegaard admits that all our talk about God
falls far short of God's greatness. Unless we are completely
silent about God, however, we must use human analogies when
we speak of God. We can measure God's greatness by human

greatness of heart, not by power and dominion. To begin to form a "conception of God's greatness, we must think of the true human greatness, that is, of love, and of the love which forgives and shows mercy." This conception of a God who is great through qualities of the heart, especially love, rather than through power and domination, implies a God closer to the traditional definition of feminine than of masculine. However, even in the midst of such a description, Kierkegaard retains the masculine pronoun to refer to God. "God's greatness lies in forgiving, in showing mercy and in this greatness He is greater than the heart which condemns itself." But Kierkegaard does confess the inadequacy of all language to describe God's greatness. "Lo, language as it were bursts and cracks under the strain of expressing God's greatness in showing mercy."[31]

In one of his communion discourses, Kierkegaard's language bursts from masculine limitations. To express the completeness of Christ's forgiveness, Kierkegaard finds the biblical image of Christ as a mother hen most appropriate:

> As when the hen concerned for her brood gathers her chickens under her wing at the instant of danger, covering them completely and ready to give her life rather than deprive them of this shelter which makes it impossible for the enemy's eye to discover them — precisely thus does He hide thy sin. Precisely thus; for He too is concerned, infinitely concerned in love, ready to give His life rather than deprive thee of thy secure shelter under His love. Ready to give His life — yet, no, it was just for this He gave His life, to assure thee of shelter under His love.[32]

Kierkegaard chooses this biblical feminine image to best describe the love of Christ that provides perfect shelter from the ravages of sin.

Foremost among Protestant theologians of modern times is Karl Barth (1886-1968). Strongly reacting against Protestant liberalism, such as that he found in Schleiermacher, Barth reaffirmed the central authority of the Word of God as revealed in Scripture and ultimately in Christ. Barth states that the only legitimate language about God is that spoken by God to the church through revelation. Barth takes the Scottish Confession's

statement of "ane onelie God" as warning against human identification with God. Barth affirms that God is personal, "but
personal in an incomprehensible way, in so far as the conception of His personality surpasses all our views of personality.
This is so, just because He and He alone is a true, real and genuine person." To conceive of God in terms of human personality
or images is to "set up the image of an idol."[33] Barth does not
realize that his masculine references to God create an image of
human personality in the minds of his readers. That Barth could
refer to the Personality who surpasses all our views of personality as "he" reveals the insidiousness of the masculine bias in
Christian theology.

Barth does, however, rise above masculine images when he
says that the only true name for God is "Thou." God is a Person, distinct from images of our imagination. God is "One Who
knows and wills, Who acts and speaks, Who as an 'I' calls me
'Thou' and Whom I can call 'Thou' in return. This is the true
name of God.... Apart from this name it would have to remain
completely hidden from us."[34] But it is the continual task of the
church to criticize and revise language about God.[35] Thus our
quest today for more inclusive language for God is in keeping
with Barth's challenge to the church.

Another influential modern theologian is Paul Tillich (1886–
1965). Tillich combined a conservative appreciation for the history of Christian thought with a desire to reformulate it in modern terms. He tried to make theology relevant to the questions
involved in human existence. One question Tillich addresses
is "whether there are elements in genuine Protestant symbolism which transcend the alternative male-female and which
are capable of being developed over against a one-sided male-
determined symbolism." In the Reformation struggle against
human mediators between God and humanity, "the female element in the symbolic expression of ultimate concern was largely
eliminated."[36] Tillich believes that this absence of female expressions of God partly accounts for the many conversions to
the Greek or Roman churches with their worship of Mary and
for the rather effeminate pictures of Jesus. Tillich recognizes
our need for fuller experience of God than what we get from
masculine language and symbols.

Tillich proposes a concept of God as "being-itself" or the

"ground of being" as one alternative to male-dominated symbolism. He says that we could avoid confusion in our doctrine of God if we understood God as first of all "being-itself." Insofar as this "ground of being" is symbolical, "it points to the mother-quality of giving birth, carrying, and embracing." This "mother-quality" of God is for Tillich the first statement that can be made about God. Using this feminine symbol of God reduces the predominance of the "demanding father-image of God."[37] Tillich, however, sees the *Logos*, as manifest in Jesus Christ, as transcending female and male through self-sacrifice:

> Self-sacrifice is not a character of male as male or of female as female, but it is, in the very act of self-sacrifice, the negation of the one or the other in exclusion. Self-sacrifice breaks the contrast of the sexes, and this is symbolically manifest in the picture of the suffering Christ, in which Christians of both sexes have participated with equal psychological and spiritual intensity.[38]

Tillich also invites us to experience the Holy Spirit as transcending male and female symbolism, even though the Bible gives us a feminine image of the Spirit brooding over chaos and bringing forth creation. Tillich thus leads us to see Christ as beyond literal maleness and the Holy Spirit as beyond literal femaleness.

Tillich believed that we must keep our doctrine of God open if it is to express the Divine Life. Barth believed that we must continually criticize and revise our God-language. As we have seen, theologians down through Christian history have struggled to describe a God unlimited by human categories. Some realized the limiting nature of masculine images of God, and some did not. In either case, a more inclusive God continued to emerge.

The work toward a Christian doctrine of God continues. It does not stop with Barth and Tillich. Our responsibility is to take insights from Christian history and to go on from here to fuller understanding and experience of God.

Questions for Discussion

1. What are some of the attitudes toward women that we find in early Christian writers? Did these attitudes influence their understanding of God?

2. How do you feel about Ambrose's image of the "womb of God the Father"?

3. What do you think Clement was trying to convey in his picture of "the care-soothing breast of the Father"?

4. Where do you see God breaking free from the male-dominated culture in which the early Christian church developed?

5. How do you explain the increase in feminine imagery for God in the Middle Ages?

6. How do you feel about Anselm's prayer to Jesus as Mother? How would you feel if you called Jesus "Mother"?

7. Which writer from the Middle Ages discussed in this chapter presents descriptions of God most satisfying to you?

8. Why did many writers during the Reformation avoid feminine images of God?

9. Which pictures of God in the book of Isaiah did Luther and Calvin find most powerful?

10. Why do you think the modern theologian Karl Barth used "he" to refer to God even as he strongly warned against thinking of God in terms of human personality or images?

11. Why do you think we resist changing our habitual language for God even when we don't agree with its implications?

12. How does Tillich help us toward a more inclusive understanding of God?

Chapter 4

Models of Change:
If God Can Include Three Persons,
Can't God Include Two Genders?

*We are indeed seeking a Trinity, but not any trinity at all,
but that Trinity which is God, and the true, the supreme,
and the only God. Keep waiting, therefore, whoever you are,
who hear these words. . . . Let us then be of this mind: so as
to know that the inclination to seek the truth is safer than
the presumption which regards unknown things as known.*

(Augustine, fifth century)

*Words and the images they convey have great power. They
can hurt and oppress or they can heal and liberate. We call
for sensitivity to the power of words. We hope for the development of language that helps and heals persons and witnesses
to the wholeness of God.*

(1984 General Conference of the
United Methodist Church)[1]

Anyone who has ever tried to explain the Christian doctrine
of the Trinity to children knows the logical problems with this
teaching. We begin with comparisons with which children are
familiar. We say, "God is like your mother, who is a wife, mother,
and teacher all in one person." But we realize the limits of this
comparison when a child asks, "Well, then if Jesus and God
are just one person, why did Jesus pray to God?" Then we try

55

another comparison. "God is like water that sometimes takes
the form of ice, and sometimes steam, and sometimes liquid
water." A bright child responds, "When water turns to ice, there
is no more liquid water. So then does that mean that when God
became Jesus on earth, there was no more God in heaven?"

If we feel frustrated by our inability to explain the Trinity,
we are not alone. The most brilliant theologians down through
Christian history have admitted their limitations as they tried to
write of one God, Creator of the universe, who at the same time
became flesh in Jesus Christ and Holy Spirit, dwelling within
believers. In their efforts to be inclusive of as much of the God of
Christian experience as possible, early church leaders developed
this doctrine of the Trinity. They realized that God escaped a
single analogy. The God revealed in Scripture and in their own
experience was more than a Father in heaven. This God was
the Word made flesh and the Spirit dwelling within, and much
more. The doctrine of the Trinity was a groping toward fuller,
deeper, more inclusive understanding of God. It was an attempt
to articulate the richness and complexity of God.

As the early church expanded its understanding of God
through the language of the Trinity, the modern church searches
for more profound insight through gender inclusive language for
God. If God can include three persons, surely God can include
two genders. Language is crucial to the way we think and experience God. Exclusive masculine language for God no longer
suffices. It limits God and human beings. As we have seen, there
is sufficient biblical and historical material with which to construct more inclusive concepts of God.

Heresy Then and Now

In an attempt to describe the God of Christian experience, the
early church wrestled for several centuries to formulate the doctrine of the Trinity. No human mind was equal to such a task.
Augustine admitted that he spoke of three persons not really
to define the Trinity, but in order not to remain wholly silent.[2]
Augustine and other church leaders who delved into the mystery of the Trinity realized how easy it was to fall into error.
They fought against any doctrinal statements that would lessen
God. Any statement that made Christ less than God was heresy.

Any view that made the Holy Spirit less than God they labeled heresy. In spite of philosophical and logical difficulties posed by the doctrine of the Trinity, they defended it against more limited beliefs about God.

Today the church is still in the process of expanding its concepts of God. Vital to this expansion is the movement beyond exclusive masculine images of God. In light of total biblical revelation, it is heresy to limit God to the masculine.

God is neither male nor female alone, but contains and transcends both. The church has traditionally affirmed this transcendence of sexuality, but at the same time used masculine language to refer to God. Thus it has resisted any concept of God that contains the female as well as the male.

We cannot call God "he" and claim that this pronoun includes female as well as male. The so-called generic "he" can be used to refer to a specific male as well as to a person of either sex, but never to a specific female. So it is not truly generic. The pronoun "he" has been used and continues to be used to exclude the female. Whether or not this exclusion is intentional, "he" does exclude the female image of God, and "he" does exclude a female human being.

A product of male-dominated culture, the church has viewed females as less than males. Concepts of God have been polluted by this prejudice, resulting in a god who is less than God. God has been created in the image of masculine human beings.

By including the female aspect of the image of God, we come a step closer to the Reality. However, a God who includes both male and female seems strange to some people. The problem, similar to that which Islam and Unitarianism have with the doctrine of the Trinity, is an overly literalistic interpretation. To the literal-minded, the Trinity is a logical impossibility at best and a three-headed monster at worst.

Modalism, one of the early Trinitarian views that the church labeled heresy, tripped over literalism. Seeing the logical impossibility in three equals one, Modalists taught that there is only one person in the Godhead, who appears at different times in three different modes. Modalists went astray in their overly literalistic interpretation of the word "persons" to describe the Trinity. Since three persons cannot be one person, Modalists could affirm only one divine Person who sometimes appears as

Father, sometimes as Son, and sometimes as Holy Spirit. When God was in the mode of Jesus on earth, then God could not at the same time be Father or Holy Spirit. Thus Modalists could not explain such biblical passages as the prayers of Jesus. The problem with Modalism is a literalism that limits God to a human understanding of personhood. It is an over-simplification of God. The church recognized the heresy in Modalism.

In formulating gender-inclusive concepts of God, we can learn the dangers of literalism from the Modalistic heresy. If we see God as moving back and forth between the forms of a male God and a female God, we have the same problems as the Modalists. We have limited God to our understanding of human personhood. A God in the female mode would be just as limited as the God confined to the masculine mode by traditional God-language.

Another danger in a Modalistic interpretation of the gender of God would be a superficial distinction of attributes according to sex stereotypes of the prevailing culture. If a particular culture views femininity as nurturing, tender, and meek, then the female mode of God would have these traits. The masculine mode of God would then be strong, protective, and authoritative. As we have seen, biblical images of God do not always conform to these stereotypes. We find strength and authority in the pictures of God as feminine Wisdom and mother bear. On the other hand, the masculine image of God is often tender and nurturing.[3] It is thus an inadequate solution to depict God in two distinct modes: the nurturing female and the protective male. More accurate to biblical revelation is the depiction of one God who includes female and male.

Some interpretations of the Trinity have sought to simplify through exclusion. One of the earliest Christian heresies was Ebionism, which excluded Christ from the Godhead. The Ebionites were Jewish followers of Jesus who avoided the logical complications of the Trinity by denying the divinity of Christ. They conceived of Jesus simply as a human being upon whom the Spirit of the Lord came. The Ebionites thus denied the eternal existence of Christ. Adoptionism, another early Christian heresy, likewise excluded Jesus from the Trinity. The Adoptionists believed that Jesus was like any ordinary human being, but at some point in his life he was adopted as the Son of God.[4]

Ebionism and Adoptionism denied the equality of Christ with God.

Instead of denying the divine nature of Jesus, Docetism excluded Jesus' human nature. The writer of 1 John alludes to the Docetists: "every spirit which confesses that Jesus Christ has come in the flesh is of God, and every spirit which does not confess Jesus is not of God" (1 John 4:2–3). Greek gnostic philosophy, which regarded spirit as good and matter as evil, influenced this Trinitarian heresy. Thus the Docetists believed that Christ could not really have come in tainted human flesh. Jesus was not a real human being, but only appeared human. The word "Docetist" comes from a Greek word meaning "to seem" or "to appear."[5]

Ebionism, Adoptionism, and Docetism all tried to simplify the Trinity by excluding the full divinity or humanity of Christ. Church councils condemned these teachings as heresy. The church should likewise condemn doctrines today that limit God by exclusion. A doctrine of God that directly states or linguistically implies a masculine God suffers from exclusion. To exclude the female aspect of God is to deny the full image of God.[6] Furthermore, to exclude the feminine image of God is to exclude important portions of biblical revelation.

To argue that we should not be concerned about the exclusion of feminine images because God transcends sexuality is to beg the question. Such an argument would logically result in the exclusion of all masculine images as well. Since, however, human understanding of personhood includes sexuality, then we are likely to conceive of the three-person God as having gender. In their preference for the masculine gender to refer to God, theologians throughout history have revealed their prejudice. Like the Docetists who could not imagine a God tainted by human flesh, Aquinas and others could not imagine a God tainted by the "female nature," which they considered defective.

This prejudice continues to play a part in the resistance to feminine images of God. Just as there were those in Calvin's day who believed that maternal images were degrading to the majesty and power of God, there are those today who feel that feminine references to God show disrespect. But instead of showing God respect through their exclusive masculine references, they diminish God by denying the feminine image of

God. By excluding the female image of God, whether in theory or in practice, the church has fallen short of the complete image of God as revealed in the biblical materials. Such exclusion of feminine images of God is therefore heresy.

Another heresy that the early church struggled to eliminate was Subordinationism. Tendencies to subordinate the Second Person and the Third Person of the Trinity took many forms. Some in the early church took the statement in John 14:26 that the Comforter "proceeds from the Father" to mean that the Holy Spirit was not co-eternal with God. This interpretation held that the Holy Spirit was a quasi-dependent, subordinate being.[7]

Subordination of the Second Person of the Trinity took the form of Arianism. In the fourth century Arius, a priest of Alexandria, taught that Christ was a created being and thus less than God. God was the only uncreated, eternal Being. Since Christ was begotten by God, Arius concluded that Christ was not God but only a quasi-divine, intermediate creature. Arianism held that this first creation of God was a superior being and the instrument of creation. This superior being was a perfect creature, but not of the substance of God. The divine nature of Christ was similar to God, but not the same. The Council of Nicea in A.D. 325 condemned Arianism as heresy, affirming that Christ was of the same substance of God and thus equal to God.[8] The Nicene Creed, however, stated that the Spirit "proceedeth from the Father," leaving ambiguous the status of the Holy Spirit in the Trinity.[9]

Subordinationist doctrines developed from a failure to understand the concept of equality within the Godhead. The Christian church, born in a patriarchal society based on hierarchy in all institutions, had difficulty formulating a doctrine of God as three equal persons. Even Origen, who was orthodox in his belief that Christ was truly God, held that Christ's inferiority to the Father was necessary to maintain the divine monarchy.[10] Problems came from such comparisons of the Trinity to hierarchical governments.

In addition, the terms "Father" and "Son" made it difficult for early theologians to think beyond the analogy of the strict hierarchy in the patriarchal family. That a son could be equal to his father was beyond comprehension. Furthermore, many of these early theologians, schooled in Greek philosophy, could not conceive of Christ as both eternal and begotten. Strict Hellenistic logic required either one or the other. The church rightly condemned such "either-or" thinking and affirmed the mystery of Christ as both begotten and eternal. The church further affirmed three equal persons in one God.

The church today can learn from the error of Subordinationism. In struggling toward more inclusive images of God, the church must guard against the subordination of female to male. The Roman Catholic veneration of the Virgin Mary reveals the inability of the church to suppress the female image of God entirely. Catholic theology, however, assigns Mary a clearly subordinate position.

As the church works toward gender-inclusive and gender-transcendent images of God, it must avoid the temptation to subordinate female to male. The designation of the Holy Spirit as feminine, though it has biblical and historical support, could lead to Subordinationism. Historical precedent for the subordination of the Holy Spirit, along with the traditional subordination of the female, could work against the Holy Spirit's equality within the Trinity. In addition, to designate one person of the Trinity feminine and two persons masculine would set up an inequality for the mathematically literal mind. Just as Arius got into problems by an overly literal interpretation of the roles of Father and Son, so a division of the Trinity according to gender presents problems. The church must thus develop a doctrine of God that affirms the equality of male and female within the equality of the three persons of the Trinity.

As we expand concepts of God, we can learn from the early church's struggle against heresy. As the early church came to the acceptance of mystery within the Trinity, so the church today must rise above a strict literalism in speculations on the gender of God. We will thus avoid the oversimplification of a Modalistic God shifting back and forth from male to female. When practical application of expanded concepts becomes complicated, we will learn from Ebionism, Adoptionism, and Docetism that exclusion is not the answer. Just as we do not have to choose between either the humanity or the divinity of Christ, we do not have to choose between either the masculinity of femininity of the Trinity. If Christ is large enough to be both human and divine and God is large enough to include three Persons, surely we can see that God is large enough to contain both female and male. We will then resist the temptation to fall back on the simplistic tradition of exclusive masculine references to God. The church can also learn from Subordinationist Trinitarian heresies the importance of equality within the Godhead. We will then avoid the traditional subordination of female to male.

The church stands at a crucial crossroad. The doctrine of God is basic to the direction the church will take. We can move back along the path of tradition, resisting new ideas and ways of speaking about God. Or we can admit and eliminate the heresy in traditional concepts of God. We can then venture forth on the ever-expanding path of gender-inclusion and gender-transcendence in our language for God.

Beyond Heresy

Biblical and historical studies have revealed that God includes and transcends male and female. Jesus said that "God is Spirit" (John 4:24), but Jesus also pictured God as male and female. Jesus called God "our Father" and compared himself to "a hen gathering her young." We too accommodate God to our understanding through use of personal references, which most often include sexuality.

Even when we acknowledge that the reality of God both includes and transcends sexuality and that all logical explanations and analogies are limited, we are still left with the practical dilemma of how to talk about God. When we use pronouns to refer to God, we immediately realize the deficiency of the English language. We do not have a singular personal pronoun that includes male and female. Because we accept the biblical revelation of one God, we cannot call God "they." Because we believe in the personal nature of God, we cannot call God "it." Until a singular personal pronoun that includes female and male enters standard English usage, we will be more accurate biblically and theologically if we refer to God as "he and she," instead of just as "he."

Most theologians today insist that God is not male, but continue to refer to God as "he." This practice is contradictory. No matter how passionately one espouses a God who is Spirit, far transcending human sexuality, masculine references convey their own meaning. Constant references to God as "Father," "He," and "King" suggest to the imagination a male God, not a spirit God. Mary Daly states that "even when very abstract conceptualizations of God are formulated in the mind, images have a way of surviving in the imagination." These masculine images "profoundly affect conceptualizations which appear to be very refined and abstract."[11] The result is a theology that implies the masculinity of God and thus the superiority of the male.

We can take the model of the church's handling of the Trinity as one alternative. In our worship services we sometimes bring all three persons of the Trinity together, as when we sing the Doxology, praising "Father, Son, and Holy Spirit." At other times we separate the three persons, singing "Father in Heaven, Who Lovest All," "Jesus, Lover of my Soul," and "Come, Holy Spirit, Heavenly Dove." Though we speak separately of the three persons, we mean the unified Godhead. We speak of one at a time while including all three.

This model will help us in our efforts to include female and male in our references to God. At times it will be appropriate to bring male and female together, referring to God as "Our Mother and Father" or as "he and she." Other times we can speak of "he" or "she" separately, while meaning both. However, it is no more acceptable to speak of God exclusively as masculine, saying we mean the feminine also, than it would be to speak only of God as Father, saying we also mean Jesus and the Holy Spirit.

Some theologians and ministers, while agreeing with inclusiveness in theory, argue that the church is not ready for practical application. They believe it would be too jarring to the majority of worshipers to refer to God as "she" or "Mother." However, those earnestly seeking to make language consistent with theology find ways of introducing inclusive God-language.

We can begin by teaching church members the wide variety of biblical images of God, the historical development of our concepts of God, and the importance of our language for God. During this transitional, informative period, we can avoid gender specific references to God entirely. Repeating the word "God" over and over in prayers and sermons, instead of using pronouns, strengthens the power and clarity of the content. In addition, we can draw from the wealth of images for God in

biblical revelation. Thus we can be true to Scripture by referring to God as "Rock," "Light," "Holy One," "Fortress," "Wisdom," "Bread of Life," "Comforter," "Nurturer," "Counselor,"
"Friend," "Sustainer," "Life-Giver," "Redeemer," "Refuge and
Strength," and so on. Using a variety of names helps us to experience the richness of God's nature and purpose and to give
witness to a God above every name.

When concepts of God grow to include male and female,
we can use masculine and feminine metaphors separately while
meaning both. In the same way, people educated in Trinitarian
doctrine can speak of the Holy Spirit, while including the other
two persons of the Trinity. A good place to begin is with female
pronouns in the context of biblical feminine images. For example in commenting on the comparison of God to mother eagle in
Deuteronomy 32: 11–12, we can say, "Like a mother eagle, God
tenderly and lovingly guides her children toward maturity. God
encourages us to grow and mature, but she remains close by to
nurture us when we are weak." Although male theologians and
preachers down through the centuries have used masculine pronouns in such a context, it is much more accurate and natural
to use feminine pronouns. In the process of expanding images
of God, a balance of female and male references is important
to break through predominant masculine concepts and then to
transcend human comparisons.

The masculine bias of the church, as well as of the English language, has fostered the easy way out in dealing with the
gender of God. As we have seen, however, through exclusive
masculine references to God, the church has fallen into heresy.
Exclusive masculine references to God are heretical in that they
are not true to the totality of God's revelation in Scripture, tradition, reason, and experience.

Seeking more inclusive language for God, the church is moving beyond this heresy. In order to fulfill God's mission in the
world, we must make our language consistent with our theology.
Language is profoundly important in biblical theology. The Bible
begins with God's speaking the world into existence. The Hebrews placed such great importance on words that God's name
was too sacred to speak. "The fact that the primary revelation
of our faith, Jesus Christ, is called the Word is the most telling
evidence for importance of language in our faith."[12] Thus to

eliminate the heresy in our doctrine of God, we must change our God-language.

Such change takes great courage and power from God. The church must have the courage to confess our sins of the past and move on to more faithful expression of God. Although inclusive language takes diligence and patience, it leads us to more profound insights and experiences of God. Then it is surely worth the effort.

Questions for Discussion

1. How would you explain the Trinity to a child?

2. Explain why Modalism was considered heresy. As we develop concepts of God that include female and male, what can we learn from Modalism?

3. How is exclusive masculine language for God similar to the early Christian heresies of Ebionism, Adoptionism, and Docetism?

4. Why do you think people continue to use exclusive masculine language for God?

5. Do you consider God, Christ, and the Holy Spirit as equal?

6. In developing inclusive concepts of God, what can we learn from the heresy of Subordinationism?

7. Why is it contradictory to say we believe that God is more than male while at the same time calling God "he"?

8. How can the church's handling of the Trinity provide a model for gender inclusive language for God?

9. How would you feel if you began a prayer with "Our Father and Mother"?

10. What do you think are the best ways of changing our language for God to make it inclusive of male and female?

Chapter 5

God-Language and Self-Esteem in Women

Do not quench the Spirit (1 Thess. 5:19).

Dear God, are boys better than girls? I know you are one but try to be fair.

(Little girl's letter to God)[1]

Biblical and historical evidence reveals that God includes and transcends male and female. Nevertheless many people cannot see the necessity for changing the way we speak of God. They insist that they can call God "he" while thinking of God as beyond gender. They do not think it worth all the effort and pain to change the language the church has used for almost two thousand years. The little girl's letter to God makes profoundly clear the importance of changing our God-language. She has internalized messages that society values males more than females. Feeling put down, she appeals to the highest authority she knows. She has been taught that God is loving and just, but male. Thus she feels the cards are stacked against her. She wonders if God can be truly fair. How can a "he" God believe girls are as good as boys?

Such an understanding of God raises a fundamental barrier to the self-esteem of women. If the supreme power of the universe is called "he," how can women believe they have as much worth as men? The church teaches women that they are created in the image of God, but then uses masculine language to refer

66

to God. This double message creates a conscious or unconscious struggle within women. Women are left wondering if they come closer to the image of God by minimizing their femininity. Masculine God-language devalues femininity by ignoring it. Women receive the subtle message that maleness, since it is used for references to God, is worthy of greater respect than femaleness. Such a message encourages women to look to men as authorities. Females who grow up with language that equates God and masculinity learn to sacrifice portions of their own identity for the approval of men. Since our theological language implies that God is male, then it is only natural that females would give males — fathers, husbands, male therapists — greater authority than they give themselves or any other woman.

There develops in many women an overwhelming need for the approval of men. Instead of looking within themselves for strength and answers, they are forever seeking male authorities to validate their worth and to tell them what to think and feel. They thus contribute to the patriarchal system of traditional psychotherapy in which "Woman as Patient learns, with the help of Man as Expert, to adapt to a situation of Father Knows Best."[2] It is easy to see how constant messages of God as male translate into messages of men as authorities in all areas of life.

Carol Gilligan's *In a Different Voice* points out that psychological theories have regarded the male as the norm and the female as deviating from this norm. Basing formulations of developmental stages on the male, Freud, Kohlberg, Erikson, and other psychologists have found females retarded in their development. Gilligan challenges these traditional patriarchal psychologies. Instead of signifying a problem in women's development, "the failure of women to fit existing models of human growth may point to a problem in the representation, a limitation in the conception of the human condition, an omission of certain truths about life."[3] Psychological models have omitted the truth of women's experience; thus they fall short of the reality of human experience.

Traditional patriarchal theology and worship have likewise presented only partial truth, that of the masculine experience of God. Thus they fall short of the reality of God and of human experience. They have contributed to low self-esteem in women by presenting the Ideal in masculine terms. If God, the Ultimate Norm, is clothed in masculine language, it is inevitable that women will feel somehow deviant. Christian writers who have labelled their comments on women in the church as the "woman problem" evidence this bias of masculinity as the norm. In religion, as in psychology, the problem lies not with women, but with the representation of the norm as masculine. The problem stems from limiting God and humanity by masculine God-language.

A theology that explicitly or implicitly fosters the concept of God as masculine contributes to feelings of inadequacy in the female. If a female accepts, either consciously or unconsciously, the notion that she is not quite as fully created in the image of God as is the male, then she will have difficulty accepting her full potential to reason and to create. Feelings of inferiority hinder many women from developing all their God-given talents.

Sharon Neufer Emswiler reveals the feelings of inferiority and alienation she experiences in a worship service in which masculine language predominates. She leaves the service feeling less human than when she came:

> That which should have created a sense of wholeness in me made me feel dehumanized, less than a full person. What was meant to be a time of worship of the true God was, for me, a worship of the masculine — the masculine experience among humans and the masculine dimension of God.[4]

Emswiler's feelings alone give us cause for changing the God-language in worship services. It is surely a sin against God's creation to make even one person feel dehumanized. But Emswiler is not a lone voice crying in the wilderness. More and more women are expressing similar feelings about exclusive masculine language to refer to God.

In *Women and Self-Esteem*, Linda Tschirhart Sanford and Mary Ellen Donovan explore some of the complex factors contributing to the low self-image of women. They indict patriarchal religions as among these factors. Protestantism, Catholicism, and Judaism have created God in the image of a male. "Every male is instantly, fundamentally affirmed by the belief that God is male, and also by the patriarchal practices that follow from it. By contrast, every female is negated."[5] Sanford and Donovan further assert that there is little doubt that women would feel better about themselves if they had grown up with powerful feminine images of God. While it is almost impossible to find women who have grown up with feminine concepts of God, there are many women who as adults have modified their ideas of God to include the feminine.

When God Is More Than Man

Sarah Granfield walked slowly into the surgeon's office.[6] For more than a year she had been agonizing over whether or not to have the gastroplasty surgery.[7] She had tried every conceivable method of losing weight, from diet pills to Weight Watchers to psychotherapy. Now she was thirty-five with two pre-school children. Her excess weight was already causing high blood pressure. Her doctor had warned her that being one hundred pounds overweight was a considerable health hazard.

So after months of soul searching and deliberation with her therapist and friends, Sarah decided to go ahead with the surgery. The surgery gave her hope of losing weight. But she still entered the surgeon's office with a great deal of fear and many unanswered questions. Her husband went along for support.

For the first fifteen minutes the surgeon addressed all his remarks to Sarah's husband. Looking at Mr. Granfield, not at Sarah, he explained the benefits and risks of the surgery. Finally Sarah had all she could take of Dr. McGuire's chauvinism. She rose to her feet in front of him and said, "Excuse me, Dr. McGuire. My name is Sarah Granfield. I've come to talk to you about surgery on *my* body. I would appreciate it if you would talk to *me* and answer *my* questions." Dr. McGuire muttered an apology and then began to talk to Sarah about the surgery.

Sarah describes what led to her ability to assert herself. She had been attending a seminar on inclusive images of God:

> In the past I might have just gone along and stifled my feelings and needs. But I have begun to see myself as a person of worth. I'm the one having surgery and my feelings matter, because I matter. The thing that's made the difference is the change that's come in my image of God. This semi-

nar has helped me see that God is just as much like me as like a man. And that makes me feel important and strong.

Unlike Sarah, professor of psychology Dr. Wanda Fielding looked and spoke as though she had never had problems with self-esteem. Trim and attractive, she sat in her university office surrounded by the symbols of her success — degrees and books. She had obviously thought a great deal about the effect of traditional God-language on women. Several years before, she had helped revise the liturgy of her church to make it inclusive in its language for God and for people. Her revision committee had even successfully changed the Lord's Prayer to "Our Father and Mother who art in heaven."

Now living in a more conservative part of the country, Dr. Fielding expressed anger over the exclusive masculine language she hears at church. In fact, she feels so strongly about the damage such language, and its underlying philosophy, does to women that she no longer goes to church. "I've ceased feeling excluded, because I've taken myself out of that realm. I feel that they're not even talking about God anymore. They're only engaging in cult rituals."

For Dr. Fielding the best metaphor for God is that of female friend. Conceiving of God in this way, she "can feel simultaneously loved and powerful. There's no trade-off between love and power. The reciprocity and mutuality of friendship best describes my relationship with God." It was clear that she had struggled through male images of God to get to this point of feeling affirmed by her relationship with God. Conceiving and speaking of God as female friend contributes to Dr. Fielding's feelings of confidence. She can feel cared for and respected at the same time.

Many women feel a deep-down sense of affirmation when they hear feminine references to God. They feel strengthened and empowered. One woman describes a feeling of increased personal identity through a closer connection with God:

Reclaiming the feminine in worship helps me reclaim myself as a person created uniquely in the image of God.... Now I know with my whole being that I am connected with God . . . and that the realization of this connection is the reason for which I was born.[8]

Rev. Deborah Hastings exults in the healing that she experiences through feminine images of God. Rev. Hastings graduated from seminary at the same time as her husband. But she was not ordained until twenty years after he was ordained, because of the external barriers of a patriarchal church and the internal struggle to claim her call. She describes the healing of built-up anger and resentment. "Internal barriers melt when I hear feminine images of God in worship. I have the same experience when receiving communion from a woman. Hard places dissolve. God is nurturing and powerful and can help us be the same."

A female college student said, "Visualizing God as female when I pray gives me strength and helps me feel that God is on my side." Other women report that inclusive God-language makes them feel "wonderful, great, reassured, strong, included, awake to the feminine dimension of God's love." One said that calling God "She," as well as "He," "Mother" as well as "Father" broadens the concept of God; it "also seems to lend more esteem to 'women's' tasks." Another would "feel that we were getting in touch with the more dynamic personality of God." One said, "I would rejoice for the liberation of *all* my brothers and sisters!"[9]

A common thread in women's comments on inclusive language is this desire for the freeing of men as well as women. Those who can include male and female in their thinking and speaking about God tend to be inclusive in race as well as gender relationships: "feminine theology takes within its embrace the human spirit in its totality."[10]

In addition, women who conceive and speak of God as androgynous or transcendent of gender tend to embrace a wide variety of interests. Their high level of creativity often takes unconventional forms.[11] They tend to associate ideas in unusual ways, and to be venturesome, aesthetically reactive, clever, and quick to respond. Progressive and original, they value intellectual and cognitive matters. Opening their minds and spirits to the diversity and expansiveness of God, these women unlock the treasures of creativity deep within themselves.

The way women conceive of God affects their level of self-confidence. The women in my research sample who see and speak of God as more than masculine scored higher in self-confidence than those whose God is masculine. Women with androgynous or gender-transcendent images of God are thus more likely to be initiators, confident of their ability to achieve goals. Feeling satisfied with themselves, they have social poise and presence. They have a high aspiration level and behave in an assertive manner. These women tend to be determined, confident, ambitious, assertive, energetic, enterprising, outgoing, outspoken, and talkative.

A profile of the women whose God is more than man also includes the traits of autonomy and dominance. High-scorers on autonomy act independently of others or of social values and expectations. They tend to be adventurous, argumentative, assertive, headstrong, imaginative, individualistic. High-scorers on dominance seek and maintain leadership roles in groups. They are strong-willed, ambitious, determined, and forceful people. Free of self-doubt in the pursuit of goals, they are inhibited little if at all by the disapproval or opposition of others.

These women whose God is androgynous or transcends gender also tend to score higher on achievement than those whose God is masculine. Hard-working and goal-directed, these individuals strive to be outstanding in their pursuits. They are determined to do well and usually achieve their goals. Their motivation to succeed seems to lie less in competitive drives than in the need to live up to high, socially commendable criteria of performance.

There is much discussion on the definition of self-esteem, and there is no definitive instrument to measure self-esteem. Work remains to be done on this elusive area of the human personality. However, it seems clear from the above descriptions of creative personality, self-confidence, autonomy, dominance, and achievement that these traits contribute to a person's overall feeling of self-worth. And as we have seen, there is a relationship between these traits in women and their ability to envision and verbalize a God who includes or transcends female and male.

When God Is Man

Unable to feel much respect for herself or for others of her sex, Frances cannot believe that the church will ever include the

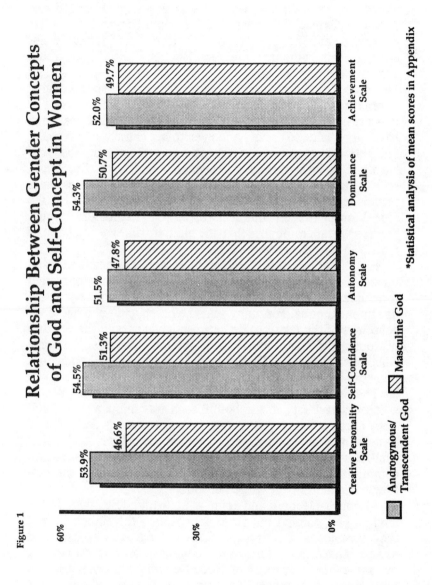

Figure 1

Relationship Between Gender Concepts of God and Self-Concept in Women

Creative Personality Scale: Androgynous/Transcendent God 53.9%, Masculine God 46.6%

Self-Confidence Scale: Androgynous/Transcendent God 54.5%, Masculine God 51.3%

Autonomy Scale: Androgynous/Transcendent God 51.5%, Masculine God 47.8%

Dominance Scale: Androgynous/Transcendent God 54.3%, Masculine God 50.7%

Achievement Scale: Androgynous/Transcendent God 52.0%, Masculine God 49.7%

Androgynous/Transcendent God Masculine God

*Statistical analysis of mean scores in Appendix

feminine in its God-language. In answer to the question, "How would you feel if God were called 'She' as well as 'He,' 'Mother' as well as 'Father,'" Frances said, "It would be nice if God were referred to as 'She' or 'Mother,' but since those terms do not elicit the same amount of respect, I doubt if the church would ever use them."

Frances' statement is sad — sad in that she has so thoroughly internalized feelings of inferiority as a woman. She has received messages, consciously and unconsciously, all her life that men have more value to society and even to her church than women. She knows that part of the resistance to calling God "She" and "Mother" is lack of respect for women. And since church and society do not place that high a value on her, Frances lacks confidence and assertiveness. On the Adjective Check List, she scored low on the self-confidence scale. So even though "it would be nice," Frances doubts that the church will ever include the female in its references to God.

Feelings of inferiority begin early in females when the Person most highly venerated is called "he." Deborah and John tried to counteract this negative influence upon their three-year-old daughter, Rhonda. For many years Deborah and John had been conscious of the relationship between language and the equality of women and men. Thus Deborah did not change her last name when she married. And they were trying to rear Rhonda in a non-sexist family.

They also wanted for Rhonda a non-sexist church. But in a conservative city in the South, such was impossible to find. They chose a church that had ordained women as deacons and pastors; no women, however, served on the church staff at that time. But they liked what they saw of the church's emphasis on community missions. Thus this church seemed to be the best they could find at this time and place.

Although Deborah and John, along with a few others in the church, had pointed out sexist language in the church liturgy, they were not taken seriously. Inclusive language was dismissed as a peripheral issue. Thus at this church Rhonda heard nothing but masculine references to God. Deborah and John tried to overcome this influence. They told Rhonda over and over again how important she was to God, and taught her to pray, "God is great. God is good. Let us thank God [not him] for this food."

One day Deborah and Rhonda were talking about God. Deborah referred to God as "she." Rhonda corrected her, "No, Mommy, God is a he." Deborah tried to explain that God was a "she," as well as a "he." Rhonda persisted, "No, that's not right. God is a he. God is a word for boys."

Rhonda is right. God has been a word for boys. Males have named God to be like them and on their side. Although only three years old, Rhonda has already picked up from church that God is for boys more than for girls. She has made such a strong connection between God and male that her own mother and father cannot convince her otherwise. The church has declared God a "he," and Rhonda has believed. To be sure, Deborah and John will continue to work against this negative influence and to affirm Rhonda in every possible way. But how much easier this would be if her church taught her that God is a word for girls as well as for boys.

From the time they are small, females suffer from exclusive masculine references to God. They internalize feelings of inferiority to men. By the time they reach adulthood, many women are not even conscious of the damage masculine references to God have done to their self-esteem. But women are becoming increasingly aware of their feelings in worship services in which all references to God are masculine. Women report feeling "excluded, unimportant, lonely, isolated, angry, cheated, tired of translating, very disappointed and hurt." One woman says she "resents the implication that God is a man." Another says that she cannot "mentally participate in the service" as much as she could if feminine references to God were included. One woman sums up the hurt she and many other women experience when she says she feels "left out, non-entity, slapped in the face."[12]

Masculine God-language contributes to women's feelings of unworthiness. Women who think and speak of God as masculine score higher on abasement than those with androgynous and gender-transcendent images of God. These women whose God is masculine tend to express feelings of inferiority through self-criticism, guilt, or social impotence. High-scorers on abasement ask for little, submitting to the wishes and demands of others and avoiding conflict at all costs. They see others as stronger, more effective, and more deserving than they.

The profile of women who conceive a masculine God includes the closely related trait of deference. These women are more likely to seek and maintain subordinate roles in relationships with others than those with androgynous and transcendent views of God. These women easily accept domination, are uncomfortable with uncertainty and complexities, and have a propensity to guilt feelings. They tend to give up and withdraw in the midst of frustration and adversity. Reluctant to commit themselves to any definite course of action, they tend to delay or avoid action, especially action involving risks.

There is a connection between the way we speak about God and the way we feel about ourselves. As we have seen, there is a statistically significant relationship between masculine concepts of God and feelings of self-abasement and deference in women. These feelings of inferiority appear to relate to their need to subordinate themselves in relationships. Deferring to a masculine God, they tend to defer to masculine human beings. Masculine God-language causes conscious and unconscious damage to the worth and dignity of female human beings. If we truly believe that male and female are created in the image of God and are equally valued in the Body of Christ, then we will change our masculine God-language that causes so much hurt.

Freeing the Spirit Within Women

As we have seen, images of God that include the feminine or transcend gender result in the increase of self-confidence, independence, and achievement in women. Women who can conceive God as more than masculine tend to feel better about themselves and to experience greater internal freedom to develop their creative and intellectual potential. Is this increase in self-worth and freedom reason enough for going to all the trouble of changing the way we speak about God? Is self-esteem a worthy goal for Christians?

The Christian church has espoused humility and self-sacrifice as virtues. Christ taught that we find our lives through losing them in sacrificial service (Matt. 16:25). However, the church has emphasized this message more for women than for men. Double standards are still alive in the church. Men are applauded for valuing themselves highly enough to achieve suc-

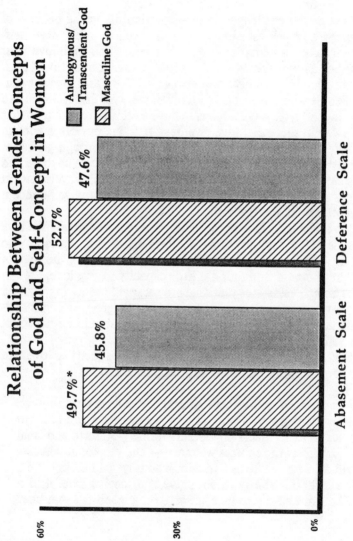

Figure 2

Relationship Between Gender Concepts
of God and Self-Concept in Women

Androgynous/
Transcendent God

Masculine God

49.7%*

45.8%

52.7%

47.6%

Abasement Scale   Deference Scale

60%

30%

0%

*Statistical analysis of mean scores in Appendix

cess. A woman who puts the same value upon herself and her work is often considered selfish and arrogant.

One of the challenges of the Christian life is the balance of humility and self-esteem. Women, as well as men, need self-esteem to live a Christian life. Christ said, "You shall love your neighbor as yourself" (Matt. 19:19). In this admonition Christ affirms the close connection between self-love and love for others. People who have trouble loving themselves find it difficult to love anyone else. A person has to have a self in order to give that self away in sacrificial love. We have to value ourselves enough to believe we have something to give. Then through giving of ourselves, we become more fully what God created us to be and thus have even more to give. We move through this cycle toward deeper and fuller "findings" of self. But a healthy self-concept is necessary at the beginning.

We are able to love because we have received love. "We love because" God "first loved us" (1 John 4:19). But, a person who has little feeling of self-worth has trouble receiving the love of God or of others, and thus has little capacity to give love. Psychiatrist Scott Peck states that "we are incapable of loving another unless we love ourselves."[13] Since Christ's greatest commandments are love of God and neighbor, there should be no doubt that self-esteem is vital to the Christian life.

Self-esteem is necessary not only for the capacity to love, but also for vocation, morality, and prophetic action:

> Our level of self-esteem affects virtually everything we think, say and do. It affects how we see the world and our place in it. It affects how others in the world see and treat us. It affects the choices we make — choices about what we will do with our lives and with whom we will be involved. It affects our ability to both give and receive love. And it affects our ability to take action to change things that need to be changed.[14]

Persons with poor self-images restrict their vocational choices by the feeling that there is little they can do well. They often adopt the attitude of the talent-burying servant whom Jesus' parable condemns (Matt. 25:14–30). In addition, they often give away their moral freedom through a deterministic attitude, a feeling that they have little power of choice. A person with a healthy self-image feels freedom in vocational and moral choices. Likewise a feeling of worth and power characterizes those people who bring about positive change. If we are to follow Christ and become the prophetic "salt and light" in the world (Matt. 5:13–14), we must believe that we are important and capable enough for God to use.

Some women protest any changes in the language of worship. They claim that they do not feel excluded or lessened in any way by references to God as "he" and themselves as "men." Exclusive language and practice have an insidious way of duping their victims. Women say things like, "Masculine references to God don't bother me. Having been brought up in that climate, I feel O.K. I don't feel uncomfortable because of life-long habit."[15] Because they have known nothing else, many women are unconscious of the damage done to their self-esteem by masculine God-language. However, more and more women are becoming aware of their feelings of exclusion and devaluation in traditional worship services.

Christian love demands that we modify our God-language to avoid damage and offense to women, whether or not they are aware of this offense. The Apostle Paul admonished the early Christians not to eat meat sacrificed to idols if this practice offended their brothers and sisters (1 Cor. 8:13). Many women are so deeply hurt by the sexist language of the church that they cannot hear the Gospel. The church would do well to heed an old Christian maxim: "those without scruples should give way to those with scruples." Those who do not think they are bothered by masculine God-language should give way to those who are.

Being included in the language of the church frees and empowers women to tap new reservoirs within themselves that in turn will enrich the whole church. The church has for too long suppressed the feminine Spirit (*Ruach*).[16] In so doing it has stifled the spiritual gifts of women. Discovering the truth of a God who includes femininity sets women free to realize their creative and intellectual potential in the image of God.

Questions for Discussion

1. How did you picture God when you were a child? What influenced this mental picture of God?

2. How do you picture God now? What influences this mental picture?

3. How does exclusive masculine language for God devalue femininity?

4. In what ways have traditional psychological theories and traditional theology ignored women?

5. Discuss ways in which concepts of God as masculine contribute to feelings of inadequacy in females.

6. Which case studies and/or quotes from women presented in this chapter can you best identify with? Explain.

7. This chapter gives the results of a survey conducted in six Christian denominations. Discuss the profile of women who think and speak of God as including or transcending female and male.

8. Discuss the profile of women who think and speak of God as exclusively masculine.

9. When we call God "he," do children picture God as male, female, or transcendent Spirit?

10. What is the connection between masculine God-language and self-esteem in girls and women?

11. Is self-esteem a worthy goal for Christian women?

12. Discuss the following quotation: "Reclaiming the feminine in worship helps me reclaim myself as a person created uniquely in the image of God."

Chapter 6

God-Language and Spirituality
in Men

*For by the grace given to me I bid every one among you not
to think of himself more highly than he ought to think, but
to think with sober judgment, each according to the measure of faith which God has assigned him.*

(Romans 12:3)

*If our spirituality cannot embrace femininity, then it re-
mains incomplete, unrealized. Spirituality in a man does
not require a denial of the feminine. On the contrary, it
is an affirmation of femininity as an essential part of ourselves — and of our God.*

(Mark Gerzon)[1]

Exclusive masculine images of God damage men as well as
women. Whereas women find reinforcement for passivity in
these masculine images, men find support for pride and control.
They are tempted to think more highly of themselves than they
ought and thus to control more than they should. Seeing God
in exclusively masculine images results in the impoverishment
of their emotional and spiritual lives.

Both explicitly and implicitly the church has taught that God
is more like a man than a woman. It is all too easy to reverse
this statement and say that man is more like God than woman.
As we have seen, Origen and other early theologians did say that
man is more spiritual than woman and thus more like God. This

kind of thinking is still with us. In 1986 a prominent leader of a major Christian denomination stated, "A woman should submit to her husband as though he were God." What stands out in this viewpoint even more than the disparagement of women is the excessive burden placed on men.

Men suffer under the load of an exclusively masculine conception of God and the accompanying patriarchal culture. In such a culture they assume the major responsibility for church, state, and home. Women who follow the advice of some Christian leaders and deify their husbands contribute to the unrealistic expectations placed upon men. If they are able to live up to these expectations temporarily, these men may develop God-complexes. When they are inevitably forced to admit that they cannot live up to such superhuman demands, they often feel incompetent or even impotent. Like Icarus, some men discover the hard way that they are not meant to fly as high as God. Gail Sheehy calls this testing of the limits of power the archetypal male fantasy. Under the illusions of this fantasy men take risks, reach higher and faster in anticipation of ascending above the heights. Then they fall under their limitations, despairing of their original dreams.[2]

Lest we think that God-complexes in men are a thing of the past, we have only to examine the not-so-subtle implications of the angry response of one man to my question concerning his feelings about including "She" and "Mother" along with "He" and "Father" in references to God. "I would feel angry — insulted — God is a male. Jesus said if you have seen me you have seen the Father. Women should be flattered to be feminine. And I don't think that they would want to be God." This man probably did not realize the extent to which he was deifying himself and other men. But on an emotional level he had made the ultimate reversal: God is male; thus male is God.

The Price Men Pay

Men suffer physically from trying to play God. The price paid for machismo is shorter life expectancy. In 1987, the life expectancy for men in the United States was seventy-two years, while it was seventy-eight years for women. The incidence of stress-related illnesses, such as heart disease, is higher among men than women. In 1985, 343 out of 100,000 men in the U.S. died from heart disease, as compared to 304 women.[3]

God-complexes in men cause emotional suffering. Shouldering a disproportionate amount of the responsibilities of society brings anxieties and fears of failures. When God is male, men get the subtle implication that they should be strong enough to handle all these pressures alone. Not wanting to reveal their vulnerability, they cut themselves off from intimate relationships. The patriarchal hierarchical marriage offers no refuge of intimacy. A one-up, one-down relationship may foster feelings of protectiveness and gratitude, but not intimacy. Equality is a necessary precondition for intimate relationships.[4] Men who try to live up to the demands of patriarchal society also cut themselves off from their children. These men lack time and emotional energy to relate closely to their children. Dorothy Dinnerstein contends that men's lack of involvement in early child care results in the stunting of their "empathic-nurturant resources."[5] Men have thus denied an essential part of their humanity.

Men suffer spiritually from exclusive masculine images of God. These images have often led them into a self-righteous lording over others. In worshipping the Lord, they really worship a masculine archetype. In so doing they form exalted images of themselves. Believing the judgment of God to be in their hands, some religious men have committed the most diabolical acts against humanity, such as witch burning.[6]

For their own spiritual wholeness, men need images of God beyond the masculine. When all references to God are masculine, men cannot feel as deeply as women the Otherness of God. "There is a deep way in which it could be natural for men to seek God through female images and women to seek God through male language, because . . . that could become a natural expression of Otherness."[7] Episcopal Bishop Paul Moore believes that the church must reflect a balance of gender for men's sake as well as for women's. Bishop Moore conjectures that one reason that more women than men are involved in church is that all our images of God are male.[8] He states, "If the objects of devotion are only male, one cannot fully experience one's own spirituality. Everyone's prayer life is impoverished if we can only relate to a male God."[9] Men, as well as women, need freedom from the constraints of a religion that equates God and male.

God Beyond Man

Dr. Phil Compton, a young business professor at a major university, balances the masculine and feminine in his concept of God and in his own personality.[10] Although Phil grew up in a conservative Southern Baptist family and church, he has always thought more in terms of God than Christ. The Father-Son image in the Trinity led to his feeling that Christ was naturally subordinate to God. Phil laughingly says, "If I wanted to pray, I'd talk to the head guy." Phil explains that he knows intellectually that the doctrine of the Trinity specifies the equality of God and Christ, but that the Father-Son image evokes a feeling of the inferiority of Christ.

Phil speaks of his own father with admiration and respect. "He's a remarkably special guy." When Phil was growing up, his father worked in the meat wholesale business. He drove around West Texas, taking Phil with him in the summer. Phil was impressed by the way his father treated the minimum-wage workers in the kitchens of the restaurants to which he delivered:

> He genuinely cared about them. He was incredibly busy. He would get up at 4:00 in the morning and sometimes wouldn't finish until 8:00 or 9:00 at night. But he would always have a kind word for the workers. When he entered the kitchens, their faces would light up. He was a high point for them, because here was someone who really cared about them. One time my dad was the only one in town who would give blood to a black child who needed an operation. He gave two pints, and then got really sick. That's a great image of God for me — someone who cares about people regardless.

Because of his experiences of the care of his mother, as well as his father, Phil can fit the "stereotypical notion of femininity, nurturing mom-type stuff" into his God framework. "Thinking of God as male and female points out in a very forceful way that it's unhealthy to put God in a box. The idea of being both male and female is something that's very difficult to comprehend, and God should be something that's difficult to comprehend." When Phil was growing up, his mother taught a Sunday School class of elderly women. Her class became a support group of fifty to sixty women. They had traumas like husbands' deaths, children's divorces, or children's drug problems. This class became a full-time ministry for Phil's mother.

It was obvious that his mother ministers to Phil as well. "My mother and I talk a lot more and on a deeper level than I do with my father. In terms of talking about life and issues and faith and religion and all that — I have most of those discussions with my mother. My mom's the absolute greatest, no question about it." Phil experiences the same intimacy in his relationship with God as he has with his mother. "I have complete openness with God, maybe even more openness than I have with my mother."

God to Phil is like his father and his mother in an "unimaginably bigger and better sense. I have a complicated picture of God. It's a picture of concern, a source of strength, perhaps a little indignation — but that doesn't threaten me. I have a sense of respect and awe for God." God, to Phil, is more Presence or Being than visual image. "Even when I was a boy, the picture of God as an old man with a long beard struck me as ridiculous."

Several of his teachers at church helped Phil see that "religion is something you can think about." When he was in graduate school, he began to see not only the power in reason, but the seductiveness of reason. "That's when I really began to understand the Faustian legend. Some university professors sell out for the academic life, just like Faust did. Their lives suffer tremendously. It occurred to me that religion isn't irrational; it's non-rational. Even reason is ultimately based on faith of some sort." The more I listened to Phil discuss his theological development, the more I was struck by how well he balances thinking and feeling in his spiritual life. So structured that he writes most of his prayers, he nevertheless speaks of God in warm images similar to those he uses to describe his mother and father.

Phil's personality corresponds to the balance of the masculine and feminine in his concept of God. He believes his personality is close to androgynous — about 55 percent masculine and 45 percent feminine. "The stereotypical male answer to a question in the business setting is, 'We should lower the price.' And the stereotypical female answer is, 'Well, I don't know, but in my opinion it seems like maybe we ought to consider lowering the price.' And I'm more that way." Phil sees himself as like women in that he considers at least two sides to every issue, instead of coming down dogmatically on one side. "It's hard for me to be certain about much of anything. I know this attitude is inconsistent with political maneuvering." Phil says that he has no need to dominate people. "I have one colleague who just scares me to death. He's a young man with a new Ph.D. He was just awful to one of the lecturers with him on a committee. He wouldn't even listen to this lecturer. He just treated her like dirt." Although Phil has plenty of self-confidence, he fears this arrogant attitude in men. "I don't want to turn into a pompous ass." Unlike some males, Phil does not attribute worth to an individual on the basis of occupational performance. And Phil eschews the traditional male authoritarian approach; instead he prefers working together with people toward a consensus. "I'm willing to give on certain issues. But I'm learning that people with strong agendas will take advantage of me."

More and more Phil is leaning toward marriage and family. "The happy, healthy home life will probably be my top priority. A warm, supportive family strikes me as the most important thing." While Phil realizes that two-career marriages can be difficult, he wants an egalitarian marriage.

A popular notion in patriarchal culture is that equality and mutuality in relationships between the sexes will somehow emasculate men. This culture has thus taught women to develop or even to feign weakness and inferiority to bolster the male ego. However, my research findings suggest that equality of gender in concepts of God and human relationships contributes positively to the male personality in some areas and does not affect it in others. Men can handle and even thrive on gender equality.

Men whose God is androgynous or gender transcendent and who believe that women should serve equally with men as ministers tend to have more confidence for risking change than those whose God is masculine.[11] These men are likely to be individualistic, imaginative, progressive, versatile, and temperamental. Perceptive and spontaneous, they tend to comprehend problems and situations rapidly and incisively. On the other hand, those men who conceive and speak of God in masculine terms only tend to be rigid, conservative, and conventional. The low-scorer on the change scale seeks stability and continuity in the environment, avoiding risky situations.

Men whose God transcends the masculine tend to be more independent and autonomous than those who hold a more traditional masculine concept of God. Assertive and self-willed, these high-scorers on the autonomy scale are interesting and arresting persons. Their profile includes adventurousness, argumentativeness, arrogance, curiosity, imagination, and impatience. Those men whose God is masculine tend to be uncomfortable with uncertainty and complexities. Their absolutist concepts of God relate to their conservative values and tendencies to judge themselves and others according to conventional standards.

Men, as well as women, benefit from gender-inclusive images of God. Equality of male and female, in heaven and on earth, does not lower the self-esteem of men. In fact, males can feel new kinds of power through androgynous concepts of God and of humanity.

Such is the experience of Ray Boyd. Ray describes feelings of freedom and power through the inclusion of the feminine in his concept of God. When he thought of God as masculine only, the expectations he put on himself burdened and stifled him. Ray used to view God as like the stereotypical traditional male: one who "gives you the high expectation and then leaves you to do it." Now he can see God as including the female who "walks with you." Because God is more than masculine, "God is able to be with me in my weakness. And the expectations that I used to put on myself as from God aren't nearly as strong. God is an understanding God who cares, who doesn't make a demand and then walk away, but who walks with me." Thinking of God as androgynous helps Ray to see that the same God who makes the demands walks beside him to fulfill them. Ray says that his picture of God and grace are now interwoven. "This view is empowering because I don't have to do everything. Now I'm freer to enjoy life. Being content with life is empowering. In my faith walk I am not so worried about being perfect as I used to be." Ray now feels relaxed and confident as he works toward his Ph.D. in psychology.

To get to this point, Ray has experienced quite an evolution in his theology. Ray's childhood picture of God separated God and Jesus. "God was a real person, masculine, angry a lot of the time. Jesus Christ was this other guy who, every once in awhile, stuck his neck out for us and got in between the guy

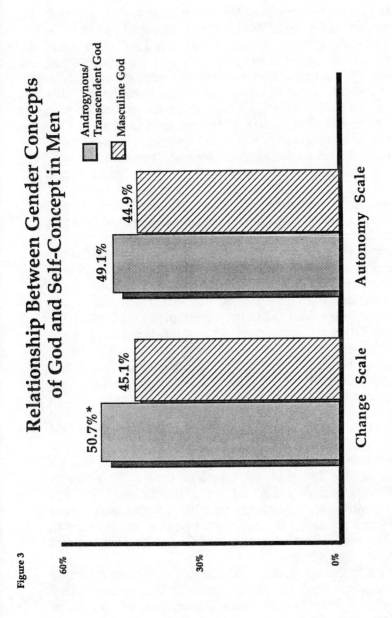

Figure 3

Relationship Between Gender Concepts of God and Self-Concept in Men

Androgynous/
Transcendent God

Masculine God

50.7% *

45.1%

49.1%

44.9%

Change Scale

Autonomy Scale

60%

30%

0%

*Statistical analysis of mean scores in Appendix

who was angry and me. And I was in trouble most of the time. I felt guilty about a lot of stuff I did. And then I would lose self-esteem." Ray says that he had many external reasons to have high self-esteem. He made good grades, was popular, and lived in an upper-middle-class family.

In college Ray still held a masculine picture of God, but God and Christ became more closely intertwined. When he was a sophomore, through a Bible study sponsored by Intervarsity Fellowship, Ray "accepted Jesus Christ as who he said he was." Soon after this experience, he was baptized. He soon discovered that "having the right interpretation of the Bible was not as important as living like Christ."

After graduating from college, Ray joined a church that challenged him to think that God might be beyond masculine. "I learned that God could handle anything I could think. Then I began to think of God more creatively." Later Ray and his wife joined an even more "progressive" church that espoused egalitarian relationships between men and women. But this church did not really challenge his view of God.

Ray's professor in a graduate course in marriage and family therapy expanded his view of God more than any "progressive" church. The professor asked, "'Is your God male or female, black or white, or what?' because he knew that this would be a starting point for how you assessed your worth. If God were male and you were female, and God was O.K., then maybe you weren't and could never be." At the beginning of this class, Ray's God was male and white. But this psychology professor exploded all Ray's preconceptions. Ray came to believe that "God is androgynous and that the most whole person is one who can be both masculine and feminine."

Viewing God as female and male has helped Ray accept the feminine and masculine within himself. He had once been afraid of his more "feminine" traits. Although boys were "supposed" to be better in math and girls in language arts, Ray "beat the socks off everybody in language arts."

This ability used to give him a feeling of "differentness, of otherness," but now he celebrates his ability to express himself verbally, along with other "feminine" qualities, such as expressing his emotions and enjoying art more than sports. Now he understands that he "can be male without doing all the peripheral things" that society labels "masculine." Accepting his masculine and feminine sides enhances his present relationship with his wife and two-year-old son. Ray feels comfortable sharing with his wife the responsibilities of making a living, child-rearing, and domestic chores.

Freeing the Spirit Within Men

A man does not have to have a masculine view of God to be a "real man." Refusing to embrace the "feminine" within God and within himself results in his emotional, intellectual, and spiritual impoverishment. He discovers wholeness when he can rise beyond stereotypical labels of "masculine" and "feminine" and accept all his traits as human.

Thinking and speaking of God as male and female frees men to accept all of themselves. If God can be androgynous, then men can be androgynous without feeling different or strange. Thus men are freed to be nurturing, emotional, supportive, and anything else society labels "feminine." Using feminine references and images in worship could give these traits more legitimacy for men, and thus help to break down our stereotypical notions of masculinity and femininity.

It is difficult for many men to take the problem of sexist language seriously. They may understand the issue intellectually, but they do not feel it on a personal, emotional level. Attending just one worship service in which the language is reversed would help. One minister confesses that he had not fully understood a female friend who felt confused and excluded by the masculine language of the church until he attended a worship service conducted with only feminine language. He says, "I certainly felt excluded. The power of words. The potency of naming."[12]

Perhaps it is hard for men to understand the problem of masculine God-language because it does not affect them as profoundly as it does women. My research discovered statistically significant differences in self-confidence, creative personality, achievement, dominance, autonomy, deference, and abasement between those women who conceive God as masculine and those who conceive God as androgynous.[13] However, for the men, the only scales affected by gender-concepts of God were change and autonomy. One of the most obvious explanations for these differences between women and men is that women feel a new sense of affirmation through inclusion of the feminine in androgynous concepts of God, whereas the male is included in both masculine and androgynous concepts of God. Thinking of God as including the feminine can help women experience for the first time that sense of affirmation and power men have always experienced through masculine images of God. There are many other possible explanations for the less measurable connections between men's gender concepts of God and self-concepts.

The negative effects of traditional God-language on men are not so obvious as they are on women. Since they have grown up hearing God called "he" just as they are called "he," they have been affirmed on a profound level over many years. They may have changed their image of God intellectually, realizing that a masculine God is not biblical or logical. Masculine images of God, however, are deeply ingrained. Thus they may say they believe that God is like both male and female or neither male nor female, but this belief has not touched them on an emotional level. When I asked for feelings about including feminine along with the masculine references to God, most of the men in my sample gave me thoughts and beliefs. They either told me why feminine references would not fit into their belief system or why they thought justice demanded including feminine references. That the issue of God's gender has not reached emotional depths in men may account for the slight effect it has on their self-image.

Men may have a tendency to express their religion through external forms such as doctrines and structured organizations, whereas women tend toward more internal, emotional experiences of religion. Perhaps then religion is not linked so closely to personality in men as in women. Men have a higher stake in institutional religion because they control a large part of it; thus much of their energy is directed to these external institutions. Women, having been excluded from institutionalized religion, are more likely to turn their spiritual energies within and find strength and sustenance in their faith. Lenz and Myerhoff observe that since women have been denied a public religious role, they "have often sought in religion a private refuge, a source of solace for personal loss and disappointment."[14]

Men within a patriarchal society may not feel the need for

God as keenly as women. Such a society teaches men to hide
their vulnerabilities and to deal with problems on their own. One
man in his late thirties said, "Men only turn to God when they
can't handle things themselves." Such feelings are the natural
result of a church and society that equate God and maleness.
Men develop God-complexes when they hear religious leaders
make statements like, "A woman should submit to her husband
as though he were God." No wonder many men come to think
they should be able to "handle" everything themselves. Women,
like blacks and other oppressed groups who have received the
message that they are not so fully in the image of God, are more
likely to turn to God for the strength they feel they lack.

Perhaps this self-sufficiency in men accounts for the fact that
they are not so regular in church attendance as women.[15] The
church through its language and leadership has given men the
message that God is male, contributing to men's feelings that
they must be strong and invulnerable. Although the church also
teaches that they are in need of God's grace, it may be hard
for men to feel this need. Thus ironically the same church that
exalts maleness drives men away.

Some men are discovering a deepening of their spiritual lives
as they expand their concept of God to include the feminine and
as they experience the ministry of women. Methodist minister
Tom Neufer Emswiler says that changing his God-language to
include the feminine has deepened his spiritual life as well as
his theological insight.[16] Perhaps the inclusion of the feminine
in religion would free men to rely on a Power Other than themselves. They may discover a deeper intimacy with a God beyond
the traditional masculine image. Just as some men are finding
that they can be more vulnerable with female than with male
ministers or counselors, they may discover the freedom to be
vulnerable before a God they can call "Mother."

Twenty-four-year-old Scott Princeton, who had been de-
pressed for over a year, experienced grace and healing through
modifying his concept of God. Scott grew up with an image
of God that closely corresponded to his experience of his father,
who remained silent and aloof when Scott tried to share his pain.
Scott felt he could never live up to his father's high standards.
Scott came to counseling with deep-seated anger toward God,
who he felt was always standing above him and judging him, like

his father. When he began to imagine God as like his mother and grandmother, he experienced release from guilt and resentment. Thinking of the feminine in God helped Scott see God as more "compassionate, self-sacrificing, sensitively caring, and open."

Some men can advocate changing God-language out of their empathy for women. Vestiges of chivalry cause them to want to "help" the women with "their problem." One man said that he felt uneasy in a worship service in which all references to God are masculine, because this language may "alienate the females present."

Men may not be aware of the extent to which masculine God-language also alienates men from portions of themselves, from others, and from God. The church has done men a great disservice by giving them only masculine images of God. Patriarchal society has taught men not to reveal their weaknesses, especially to other men. Therefore when God is male, they cannot be completely open and honest even with God. Just as a dominant position in marriage alienates husbands from wives and deprives them of intimacy, so a dominant position in the church deprives men of the wholeness that comes from mutuality and intimacy within a faith community. Men become overburdened and pressured by superhuman demands of leadership. Men can thus go beyond good intentions to change the masculine language and structure of the church for women's sake. Changes need to come for men's sake as well.

Surely the language of the church does not have to exclude female or male. Men, as well as women, find power and wholeness through including the feminine in worship language. One young man says that he would feel "great" if God were called "She" as well as "He," "Mother" as well as "Father." He goes on to say, "I've participated in some inclusive language liturgies and have found them quite powerful. God is our Mother too and I pray to Her as such."

Discovering dimensions of God beyond the masculine could release men to discover new depths within themselves and to experience a deeper spirituality. When God is called "Mother" as well as "Father," men, along with women, will become more fully the image of God. The church owes men this opportunity to be all God created them to be.

Questions for Discussion

1. How do you feel about the statement made by a leader of a Christian denomination: "A woman should submit to her husband as though he were God."

2. How does masculine language for God contribute to the dominance of men in church and society?

3. In what ways do men suffer from the heavy expectations placed upon them because of implications that God is male?

4. Discuss the following quote from Bishop Paul Moore: "If the objects of devotion are only male, one cannot fully experience one's own spirituality. Everyone's prayer life is impoverished if we can only relate to a male God."

5. Which case studies and/or quotes from men presented in this chapter can you best identify with. Explain.

6. Discuss the profile, resulting from the survey, of men who think and speak of God as including or transcending male and female.

7. Discuss the profile of men whose God is exclusively male.

8. Does including the female in their concepts of God lower the self-esteem of men?

9. Why is it difficult for many men to understand sexist language as a problem?

10. How do you explain the less measurable connections between concepts of God and self-concepts in men than in women?

11. How do you explain the fact that fewer men than women are involved in church?

12. What do men have to gain from inclusive language in church ?

Chapter 7

God-Language and
the Church's Future

*There is neither Jew nor Greek, there is neither slave nor
free, there is neither male nor female; for you are all one in
Christ Jesus.* (Galatians 3:28)

*When women name the holy — not just in themselves, but
in all those different elements that the historical fact of being
female gives them a chance of confronting or understanding — they are not just making themselves feel better, they
are giving the Christian community a God-gift.*
(Sara Maitland)[1]

The way we conceive and speak of God has profound implications. As we have seen, our conceptions of God influence our
conceptions of ourselves. These conceptions carry over into the
ways in which we organize all of life, including our religious
institutions. Masculine images of God and male-dominated religious institutions go hand in hand.

Worship of God has been controlled by men. Men have created a masculine God in their own image. This male God then
serves as the most powerful sanction for an all-male priesthood.
If God is masculine, then only males can represent God in worship. That this theology undergirds the all-male priesthood in
the sacramental traditions is understandable. It is much more
difficult to explain the all-male pastoral leadership that developed within the free church, which espouses the priesthood of all

believers, male and female. Exclusive male pastoral leadership contradicts the doctrine of the priesthood of the believer. The result in both sacramental and free church traditions has been the stunting of female gifts and the maiming of the collective Body of Christ.

Although the Bible does not restrict the gifts of the Spirit by gender, the church has traditionally set such restrictions. Of the five gifts Paul lists in Ephesians 4:11, women have been denied the use of four. The church has not allowed them to be apostles, prophets, evangelists, or pastors. And when pastor-teacher is viewed as one gift, as the syntax of the verse in the original Greek language implies, women are totally excluded from the exercise of the gifts listed in this passage. Not only has the spiritual growth of women suffered from this exclusion, but the spiritual life and growth of the entire Body has suffered. Paul Jewett states that if Christian men "cannot empathize with women in this problem, let them reflect upon what it has cost the church, of which they are the leaders, to use only the tithe of its female talent."[2]

Gender of God and of God's Ministers

People who can imagine and verbalize an inclusive God are likely to be inclusive in their views of God's ministers. If God extends beyond the masculine, then God's representatives do not have to be male. People who avoid sexism in their language about God tend to avoid sexism in their views of ministers.

My research revealed striking relationships between beliefs concerning the gender of God and the gender of ministers. Of the entire sample of 174 men and women, approximately 91 percent of those with a concept of God as androgynous or transcendent believe churches should ordain women and give them opportunities to serve as pastors or priests and as deacons, as contrasted with 69 percent of those with a masculine concept of God.[3] The connection between views of God and ministers was even more pronounced among Roman Catholics. In this largest of Christian denominations approximately 83 percent of those with an androgynous or transcendent view of God, as contrasted with only 25 percent of those with a masculine view of God, believe women should serve as priests.

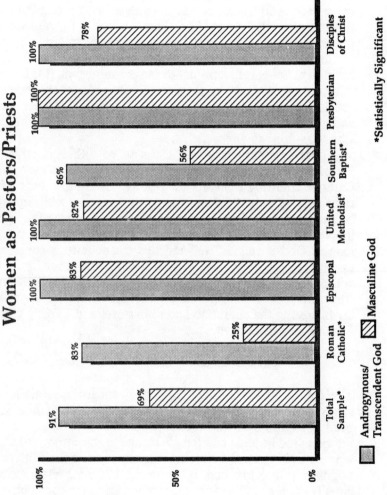

Figure 4

Percentage Open to
Women as Pastors/Priests

100%

50%

0%

Total
Sample*

Roman
Catholic*

Episcopal

United
Methodist*

Southern
Baptist*

Presbyterian

Disciples
of Christ

91% 69% 83% 25% 100% 83% 100% 82% 86% 56% 100% 100% 100% 78%

▨ Androgynous/
Transcendent God   ▨ Masculine God

*Statistically Significant

The gender of God profoundly affects the gender of God's ministers in the Catholic tradition. The Vatican has declared that there must be a "natural resemblance" between Christ and the person who offers the sacraments. If a woman performed this priestly role, "it would be difficult to see in the minister the image of Christ. For Christ himself was and remains a man."[4] In the Catholic tradition, the sex of God and Christ is not a peripheral issue. It determines the sex of ministers. It is obvious that this official Catholic position places gender as the foremost consideration in the "image of Christ." For surely Mother Teresa and many other women have reflected the spiritual image of Christ as fully as any male priest.

Those denominations that claim to base their doctrine on Scripture alone actually derive ordination practices more from Catholic tradition than from Scripture. Even those denominations that vehemently denounce papist practices are influenced by the Roman Catholic sacramental concept of priesthood and hierarchical church polity, more than they want to admit. As long as God is called "He" and this masculinity is considered essential to the person of Christ, Catholics and other Christians will have difficulty giving women full recognition as God's ministers. Freeing God from human concepts of masculinity will go far in freeing the church to accept pastoral and priestly gifts of women as well as men.

When God and Humanity Are Liberated

The church has everything to gain by inclusive thinking and speaking of God. Concepts of God, as well as of humanity, need liberation from patriarchal exclusiveness. As we have seen, viewing God as male and female results in the empowerment of women and men and in freeing them to exercise their full range of gifts within the church. When sisters and brothers participate equally in spiritual leadership, profound and beneficial changes will take place.

The inclusion of women will result in changes in the organizational structures of the church. Church polity has been hierarchical with men at the top. These hierarchical structures suppress the gifts of both women and men. Women and all but the few men at the top have little power in decision-making.

Real power rests in the hands of only a few men even in those churches that pride themselves on their democratic polity. This results in a "let-the-paid-leaders-do-the-work" mentality and thus a loss of the creative gifts of the majority.

Rosabeth Moss Kanter, adviser to some of the most influential companies in America, believes that the empowerment of greater numbers of people within organizations produces greater commitment and creativity.[5] Such empowerment of individuals should have originated in the church, not secular organizations. The Christian church has historically professed the belief that each member is gifted and empowered by the Holy Spirit (1 Cor. 12:7-14). Yet its hierarchical organizational structure keeps the empowerment of members an ideal rather than a reality. The spiritual power and gifts of all members will be released only through the breaking down of rigid hierarchies.

One important contribution women can make to the church is an alternative organizational model. Women lean toward mutuality and networking rather than hierarchy. Women can offer the church a model of mutual ministry that is "more supportive of the talents of all the individuals concerned, more open to change, and more loving of the individual members of the organization."[6] Those denominations that have been supportive of women in the ordained ministry have seen creative changes in leadership, such as a male and female serving as co-pastors who share equally in preaching, counseling, and all other pastoral responsibilities. This sharing of pastoral ministry presents a model of mutual ministry for the entire congregation to follow. Women pastors tend toward less distinction between laity and clergy, giving laity more power in decision-making. As one female pastor said to a group of women, "We have to have power in order to give it away."

An ordained Southern Baptist woman, as she was about to assume her first position as senior pastor, expressed her conviction that pastors are not to dictate to people, but rather to encourage and empower people to be equipped to be the servants of God. "I feel very strongly that we need to listen together as a community to what way we might go together." Her hope is that women "can encourage some new visions for pastoral leadership and the way to be church." She believes that women can contribute a style of leadership not interested in domination and control, but rather in discernment of the direction the Spirit moves the whole community. She says, "I seek empowerment for the whole church."[7]

Women especially seem to gain a new sense of worth and power from a female pastor. A member of a United Methodist church says about her pastor, "She makes me feel like I can do more than I ever thought I could. She even got me to lead a worship service in a nursing home." This member of the church for almost fifty years has seen close to twenty pastors come and go, all of them male before the present pastor. "She has a warmth and real concern for people that comes through in all that she does. She is a strong leader. But there is a difference in her leadership. It's hard to describe the feeling she gives me, but I know she really cares about people. It's obvious from the way she preaches, presides over board meetings, and especially when I'm just talking with her one-on-one."

Women are changing the leadership structures in the Episcopal church as well. One woman priest who has served as senior rector of an Episcopal church since 1981 describes her leadership style as "one which involves leaders of the church and empowers people to do their own ministry. I believe in a participatory type of government, not an authoritarian one." A retired man, a member of this church for fifteen years, finds the pastoral leadership of the church's first female rector "diametrically opposite to that of the former rector. He was quite autocratic. It was his church and he ran it. She prefers to work through committees. Her modus operandi is to get as many people as possible involved in any activity. She works through people instead of going it alone." She recalls being interviewed for the rectorship: "When they interviewed me, I was up front with them about the style of leadership I would employ. They were very pleased and eager to become involved in the running of the church, and it has worked well. This kind of leadership is a growing part of our theology. We believe everyone has a ministry and that the church should assist people in identifying their gifts for ministry, train them, and affirm them to do ministry."

The empowerment of women and men for ministry will lead to more harmonious relationships among men and women. Antagonism between the sexes is evidenced by the divorce rate, pornography sales, and sexual violence. The traditional subordination of women to men contributes to such alienation and exploitation. Patriarchal religion has served as a powerful sanction for this subordination. Men who have had to carry the weight of church and state often blame the women closest to them for their failures to live up to these unrealistic expectations. Women who have had to look to men for their identities and their very survival often blame them for their lack of fulfillment. Alienation and divorce often result from this dominant-submissive pattern in marriage relationships.

From this pattern also comes the view of man as subject and woman as object, resulting in the abuse of women through pornography and violence. A woman whose religious tradition has taught her to be submissive finds it difficult to leave an abusive relationship. After all, she has been taught to "submit to her husband as though he were God." Men from these traditions may carry to the extreme what their churches have taught them about God as male and themselves as "head," justifying mental and physical abuse of women.

Abused women, as well as their abusers, need non-masculine images of God. Some women have had such devastating experiences with fathers and husbands that male references to God lead them to reject God and the church altogether. A counselor at a family abuse center states that a high percentage of the women who come to the center are "very anti-male. And since they are referring to God as a man and it was a man who abused them, their feelings of not liking God are intensified. That is probably a very big factor in why some do not stay involved in church, because God's a man, and that preacher up there's a man and their abuser's a man."

Susan Weidman Schneider points out the alienating results of excluding the female aspect of God from religious liturgy. She finds in Jewish mysticism the importance of the female *Shekhinah*, the divine presence manifest on earth. The exclusive masculine language referring to God in liturgy tears asunder the male and female aspects of God. This alienation of the masculine and feminine in God results in the exile of women from the religious community. Reuniting the masculine and feminine in liturgy will bring the female half of humanity from exile and will begin reparation.[8] Such a reuniting is sorely needed in the Judaeo-Christian tradition. Religious institutions that in the past have contributed to brokenness and oppression will then be converted to models of liberation and wholeness.

When God is freed from masculine language and stereotypes, many women who have felt alienated from God and the church will return. A woman studying for a graduate degree in English left her church after thirty-five years of active membership because she could "no longer believe in a masculine God and male-dominated church that puts down half the human race." The lack of female representation caused a minister's daughter to drop out of church: "The church taught me that God was loving, that God loves everyone just the same. But then women weren't allowed to take important leadership roles in the church. That just didn't compute." Women experiencing inclusive worship for the first time report feelings of great release and renewed connection with God and the community of believers. One young woman says, "I could talk to my mother about anything. That's why the image of God as mother was so life-giving to me."

The equal participation of women in church leadership, resulting from inclusive images of God, will bring greater unity to the Body of Christ. Exclusive male leadership has created rigid denominational structures that often become barriers to unity and cooperation among Christians. Women more readily cross denominational lines in the interest of common causes. Such groups as Church Women United and Evangelical Women's Caucus evidence the strength of women's ecumenical efforts. In seeking opportunities to exercise their calling, women have embraced ecumenical ministries and have accepted positions in denominations other than the one that ordained them. Women tend to replace the "either-or" positions of patriarchal religious institutions with "both-and" perspectives. The struggle for the inclusion and celebration of the feminine experience brings together women of many different faiths. Women will contribute to the church as a whole a spirituality that is "integrative rather than divisive, crossing over the sectarian boundaries of traditional religions."[9]

Including the feminine in concepts of God and including women in church leadership will contribute to peacemaking efforts. Traditionally women have been protectors and nurturers of life both within the church and the larger human community. Today when churches are being torn by doctrinal battles and when the world hangs in precarious balance between superpowers capable of setting off nuclear holocaust, we can afford no longer to ignore the peacemaking gifts of women.

Doctrinal controversies in major Christian denominations have become divisive and political. While the conflict may be most visible in the Southern Baptist Convention, other mainline denominations have also suffered. The fundamentalist battle over the inerrancy of the Bible is led by men, not by women. In the first place, the fundamentalists use literalistic interpretations of certain Pauline passages to keep women out of leadership. In the second place, the controversy has the more "masculine" emphasis on external structures, on doctrinal conformity, and on rationalistic theories of the inspiration of Scripture. Women's internal, unifying type of religion continues to find expression in mission organizations. While men are arguing over verbal plenary versus dynamic theories of inspiration of Scripture, women are gathering support for mission causes. In a meeting of Southern Baptists in the fall of 1987, a leader of Woman's Missionary Union called for reconciliation and unity through support of the broader mission of the church, spreading the Gospel throughout the world.

An emerging group of clergywomen within mainline denominations contributes a model of peacemaking for the entire Christian community. These women have made personal and professional sacrifices to remain within religious institutions that merely tolerate or openly reject them. Some people think these clergywomen are crazy not to split off from traditional churches or to enter professions where their talents would be more fully recognized and rewarded. A wide range of feelings, from loyalty to prophetic zeal, keeps these women within traditional structures, persistently working for change. Instead of declaring war, they adopt peaceful means of change through the power of truth and love.

Increased leadership opportunities for women will thus enhance the church's peacemaking efforts in the world. Women have a history of involvement in peace movements. Beginning in 1854 with the formation of the Women's Peace League in Europe, women have given birth to numerous peace organiza-

tions, such as the Women's International League for Peace and
Freedom, Women Strike for Peace, Peace Links, and Women's
Action for Nuclear Disarmament. Women readily unite their
efforts and talents with those of men in groups such as World
Peacemakers, Psychologists for Social Responsibility, and Physi-
cians for Social Responsibility. For almost ten years, Dr. Helen
Caldicott has been a leading spokesperson for the physicians'
group.

When the church includes feminine along with masculine
metaphors for God and when women participate equally in
leadership, peacemaking will become a higher priority in the
church. If we can recover the Genesis metaphor of a female
Spirit (*Ruach*) active in creation, then we can more fully identify
God with women's concern for nurturing and preserving life. A
lay Franciscan, active in peace and justice movements, remarks,
"As long as I let people put the image of God as father in my
mind, I had trouble seeing the nurturing aspects of God. My father was a provider, but not a nurturer." Female images of God
bring greater value to the role of peaceful preservation traditionally assigned to women, and could thus lead more men to feel
that peacemaking deserves their best efforts. Imagining God as
a nurturing, peace-loving maternal figure will help liberate and
inspire men and women alike to assume greater responsibility
for preserving creation.

The church that limits God by masculine references and
limits the ministry to males quenches the Spirit. Instead of empowering every member of the Body of Christ for ministry, the
church has stifled the gifts of women and men through rigid
assignment of gender roles. Through emphasizing roles instead
of gifts, the church distorts the biblical message. Members have
gifts, not roles, "that differ according to the grace given to us."
We are to "earnestly desire the higher gifts," not the proper
roles.[10]

We have only begun to glimpse the transformation that will
come when gender no longer restricts our concepts of God and
of humanity. The church stands on the verge of a second reformation, a reformation that will come through expanding the
ways we think and speak of God. Women and men will then
have opportunities to serve equally. Encouraging all members
to find and use their unique gifts will bring the church closer

to its potential as an agent of reconciliation, peace, unity, and empowerment.

Theology and ecclesiasticism are closely intertwined. Concepts of God shape church polity and mission. God-concepts and God-language are inseparable. Calling God "He," "Father," and "King" provides powerful sanction for a patriarchal, hierarchical church. A masculine God reinforces male ministers as the norm, making female ministers appear an aberration at worst and the exception at best. Experiencing a psychological incongruity between a masculine God and a female minister, some people argue against women in the pastorate because "it is just not natural." As we have seen, most people who can include the feminine or go beyond gender in their concepts of God have no trouble accepting women as pastors and priests.

In a world of divisions and brokenness, the church can bring wholeness. In the world, and unfortunately in the church as well, we divide ourselves into groups: rich and poor, male and female, black and white, clergy and laity, normal and handicapped, young and old. A masculine God reinforces divisions and exclusivity. A masculine God encourages other kinds of exclusion, such as racial and economic. Creating God in the image of a white, middle-class male supports the continued exclusion of a large proportion of humanity from opportunity and power.

The church today struggles in the midst of the crisis of internal conflicts and diminishing membership. If the church takes this crisis as an opportunity to liberate God and humanity from the clutches of patriarchy, it has a bright future. If the church refuses to change, it will become archaic and superfluous. The church must choose whether it wants to be exclusive or inclusive, selective or universal. The language we use for God reflects our choice and thus has profound implications for the future of the church. Through inclusive God-language, the church can model justice and become a dynamic, prophetic voice within our world community.

Questions for Discussion

1. What do you think the church has missed by limiting the ministry of women?

2. Discuss the results of the research on the relationship between beliefs concerning the gender of God and the gender of ministers.

3. In what Christian denomination is the connection between views about God and about ministers most pronounced? Explain.

4. What positive changes in the church will result from inclusive thinking and speaking about God?

5. How is sexist language related to the high divorce rate, pornography, and sexual violence?

6. In what ways has the church stifled the gifts of women and men through rigid assignment of roles according to gender.

7. How does calling God "He," "Father," and "King" reinforce male ministers as the norm?

8. How would you feel if you called God "She" as well as "He," "Mother" as well as "Father"?

9. How would you feel about having a woman as your pastor or priest?

10. In what ways will inclusive language and ministry help the church become a prophetic voice within our world community?

Epilogue

Beyond God as Male and Female

While several Christian denominations continue to debate the ordination of women, others have moved on to shake the foundation of patriarchy in the doctrine of God. Realizing the connection between God-language and patriarchal institutions, inclusive language task forces in various denominations propose revisions of hymnals and lectionaries. For many years the National Council of Churches has been considering the authorization of an inclusive language translation of the Bible.

These proposed changes evoke varied, often intense responses. Some view inclusive language as a peripheral issue. One young man believes that those who advocate balancing masculine with feminine God-language "are making a whole lot out of nothing." He further states, "I can't see how we can even remotely grasp of God as Creator of the Universe and then try to limit Him to a strict male or female role." This man was totally unaware that he was limiting God to a male role by referring to God as "Him." A middle-aged man reacted more strongly: "Anyone trying to categorize God as male or female has such a small mind, they must have a rather limited picture of a limitless being. God's sex is no more important than his height, weight, or skin color. He, in fact, has none of the above. Concern over God's sex is petty and inane."

In reacting against feminine language for God, these people present powerful arguments against masculine language for God as well. If they believe that categorizing God by gender limits God, then surely they would not call God "he." If the gender of

God is so unimportant, then they should have no more problem referring to God as "she" than as "he." In reacting so strongly against feminine references to God, they reveal the ancient bias that women are inseparable from their sexuality. Calling God "she" brings up the issue of God's sex in ways that calling God "he" never has. Since the church has explicitly and implicitly taught that men are more spiritual than women, it has allowed men to rise above their carnality to perform the sacred rituals, while keeping women tied to the flesh. Therefore, a "she" God might not be worthy of worship. A "she" God would be no God at all to some people. If God is She, God is not God.

Although the church has traditionally afforded masculinity more honor than femininity, a "he" God is likewise limited by human gender stereotypes. If God is He, God is not God. Exclusive masculine references to God restrict God to human understandings of gender. Although some argue that the pronoun "he" is generic, the predominant images and traits it evokes in the mind are masculine, since it also serves as a specific reference to a male. Furthermore, as generic terms pass out of standard English usage, the argument for masculine references to God will continue to lose credibility.[1] The generic "he" derives from patriarchal society, which determines masculinity as the norm and even projects masculine gender onto God. However, a God confined to one human gender could never be the infinite, almighty God whose thoughts are not our thoughts and whose ways are not our ways (Isa. 55:8).

As we have seen in this study, neither the Bible nor Christian history limits God to the masculine gender. The Bible presents a remarkable variety of divine metaphors, many of them feminine. Using language that creates only a masculine image of God is unbiblical and idolatrous. Leading theologians throughout the centuries have risen above the bias of their milieu to offer glimpses of a God larger than masculine gender. From St. Ambrose's "womb of God the Father" to Tillich's "ground of being," we discover the possibility of progressing beyond gender concepts of God by including male and female. Just as the early Christians' experience of God demanded the expansion of God-language to include three Persons, so we can describe more fully and enlarge our experience of God through language that includes both genders.

My study has revealed that inclusive God-language has profound implications for the Christian church. This language frees and empowers women and men to exercise their gifts within the church. Women gain the self-confidence and autonomy to achieve, create, and lead. Men discover deeper capacities for spirituality, intimacy, and change. The church gains wholeness and redemptive power through the mutuality of men and women in leadership and ministry. As the church breaks down rigid hierarchies and roles, it gains the contributions of each unique member. When the church values women and men equally, it becomes a model of justice and peace.

Although some advocate a time of exclusive use of feminine references to God to balance the centuries of masculine God-language, my emphasis has been on expanding and enriching our doctrine of God through inclusive language. Changing the nature of the limitation upon God from masculine to feminine would be no permanent solution. However, including male and female in our metaphors for God offers fuller understanding of God and greater wholeness for humanity. Since human beings come in the form of one gender or the other, speaking of God as including both genders contributes to a doctrine of God beyond humanity. Calling God "she" focuses on the metaphoric nature of our language for God in ways that calling God "he" does not, because masculine references have become habitual. Feminine references jar us out of habits inconsistent with our theology. Balancing masculine and feminine references to God leads the imagination beyond anthropomorphism to a transcendent God. In addition, speaking of God as male and female provides a powerful affirmation of male and female human beings.

As we have seen, it is not sufficient to use masculine God-language and argue that it is generic, not specific; analogical, not literal. There is no way we can expound a doctrine of God as transcendent Spirit and use only masculine references to God. We simply cannot have it both ways. My study intentionally overemphasizes the gender of God. But we have to focus upon the gender of God in order to transcend it. The way to a God beyond male and female is through a God who includes male and female. The imagination can more easily leap from androgynous to transcendent concepts of God than from masculine to transcendent concepts of God.

Just as the day will come when female pastors are called simply "pastors," not "women pastors," the day will come when the gender of God ceases to be an issue. Through speaking of a God inclusive of male and female, we will progress to deeper understandings of God beyond male and female. We will then experience more fully the power of God and the glory of being female and male in the image of God.

Appendix A

Religious Opinion Survey

The questions that follow, along with "The Adjective Check List" by Harrison G. Gough, made up the survey for chapters 5–7 of this book.

Answers to questions 6, 9, 10, 12, 13, 18, and 20 determined the classification of respondents into two categories. Those who chose masculine terms on at least four of the questions were placed in the masculine God category. Those who chose both masculine and feminine or neither masculine nor feminine on at least four of the questions were placed in the androgynous/transcendent God category. None of the respondents chose the exclusive feminine terms.

Questions 15 and 17 determined the respondents' openness to ordained women serving as pastors/priests and deacons.

Answers to questions 22 and 23, along with personal interviews, provided illustrations for chapters 5–7.

1. Christian churches today need more...

    a. evangelistic outreach
    b. spiritual depth
    c. social ministries
    d. enthusiastic worship

2. I believe God is...

    a. a concept too difficult to grasp
    b. a personal friend
    c. a crutch for weak people
    d. an indifferent ruler of the universe

3. The most important function of a church is...

    a. to provide social services
    b. to aid people in their search for God
    c. to help people get to heaven
    d. to teach people the Bible

4. I believe God is...

    a. just
    b. merciful
    c. neither just nor merciful
    d. both just and merciful

5. My concept of God...

    a. has remained the same for as long as I can
       remember
    b. has changed in the past ten years
    c. has changed in the past five years
    d. changes from day to day

6. I believe God is like...

    a. a male
    b. a female
    c. neither male nor female
    d. both male and female

7. I believe God is...

   a. judgmental

   b. forgiving

   c. neither judgmental nor forgiving

   d. both judgmental and forgiving

8. When I think of God, I feel...

   a. afraid

   b. loved

   c. confused

   d. overwhelmed

9. God should be called...

   a. Father

   b. Mother

   c. neither Father nor Mother

   d. both Father and Mother

10. The Bible presents God as...

   a. feminine

   b. masculine

   c. neither masculine nor feminine

   d. both masculine and feminine

11. After death a person...

   a. ceases to exist

   b. becomes reincarnated

   c. goes to heaven or hell

   d. continues to exist in some way

12. Christian theologians have conceived of God as...

    a. masculine
    b. feminine
    c. neither feminine nor masculine
    d. both feminine and masculine

13. God should be referred to as...

    a. It
    b. She
    c. He
    d. both She and He

14. I believe God is...

    a. demanding
    b. nurturing
    c. neither demanding nor nurturing
    d. both demanding and nurturing

15. As pastors and priests, Christian churches should ordain...

    a. men
    b. women
    c. neither men nor women
    d. both men and women

16. Hymns, readings, and sermons used in Christian worship should delete...

    a. militaristic language
    b. sexist language
    c. neither militaristic language nor sexist language
    d. both militaristic and sexist language

17. In Christian churches women should have opportunities to serve as...

    a. pastors/priests
    b. deacons
    c. neither pastors/priests nor deacons
    d. both pastors/priests and deacons

18. I believe God is...

    a. feminine
    b. masculine
    c. neither feminine nor masculine
    d. both feminine and masculine

19. To Christian ministry, God calls...

    a. women
    b. men
    c. neither women nor men
    d. both women and men

20. When I picture God in my mind, I see...

    a. a man
    b. a woman
    c. neither a man nor a woman
    d. both a man and a woman

21. Do you think you are more responsible for the ongoing of the church than a person of the opposite sex? Explain.

22. How do you feel in a worship service in which all references to God are masculine?

23. How would you feel if God were called "She" as well as "He," "Mother" as well as "Father"?

Appendix B

Statistical Analysis of *t* Tests

WOMEN

Creative Personality Scale
$t(115) = 4.23, p < .0001$

Self-Confidence Scale
$t(104) = 2.09, p < .04$

Autonomy
$t(113) = 2.40, p < .02$

Dominance
$t(115) = 2.76, p < .01$

Achievement
$t(115) = 1.80, p < .08$

Abasement
$t(111) = -2.79, p < .01$

Deference
$t(115) = -3.24, p < .002$

MEN

Change
$t(55) = 2.28, p < .03$

Autonomy
$t(55) = 1.80, p < .08$

Notes

Introduction

1. Sharon Neufer Emswiler and Thomas Neufer Emswiler, *Women and Worship* (San Francisco: Harper & Row, 1974), pp. x–xi.
2. John Bertram Phillips, *Your God Is Too Small* (New York: Macmillan, 1960), pp. 1, 38.

Chapter 1: The Bible and How We Read It

1. All biblical references are to the Revised Standard Version, unless otherwise noted.
2. The terms "Old Testament" and "Hebrew Bible" are used synonymously.
3. C. S. Lewis, *Reflections on the Psalms* (London: Collins, 1958), p. 22.
4. Ibid., p. 94.
5. The first word for God in the Bible, *Elohim* (Gen. 1:1), a plural form, seems to be derived from an ancient Semitic female god, *Eloah*, and a male god, *El. Ruach*, the Hebrew word for Spirit, is feminine in form.
6. *An Inclusive Language Lectionary: Readings for Year A* (New York: National Council of Churches of Christ in the U.S.A., 1983), p. 1.
7. The Revised Standard Version has a footnote indicating that "begot" can also be translated "bore." The Hebrew verb can mean either the begetting of the father or the bearing of the mother. The Hebrew verb translated "gave birth" describes a woman in labor and never refers to the action of a man. Thus the predominant image in this verse is of God as a woman giving birth.
8. Revised Standard Version of the Bible (New York: National Council of Churches of Christ in the U.S.A., 1946, 1952), p. viii.
9. See chapter 2, "The Unlimited God of Scripture," for a discussion of feminine images of God in the Bible.

10. Patricia Gladney Holland, "In the Presence of the One Who Comforts Us as One Whom a Mother Comforts," *Journal for Preachers* 10 (Pentecost, 1987), p. 11.

Chapter 2: The Unlimited God of Scripture

1. Leonard Swidler, *Biblical Affirmations of Woman* (Philadelphia: Westminster Press, 1979), p. 35.

2. Phyllis Trible, *God and the Rhetoric of Sexuality* (Philadelphia: Fortress, 1978), p. 51.

3. Virginia Ramey Mollenkott, *The Divine Feminine: The Biblical Imagery of God as Female* (New York: Crossroad, 1983), pp. 89–90. The image of God as mother eagle also occurs in Exod. 19:4: "You have seen what I did to the Egyptians, and how I bore you on eagles' wings and brought you to myself." As the mother eagle takes her young on her wings to teach them to fly on their own, so God led the children of Israel out of Egypt to freedom and independence.

4. Trible, *God and the Rhetoric of Sexuality*, pp. 52–53. See also Trible's parallel of this passage with Jeremiah 31:20, along with her thorough discussion of the metaphor of the God of the womb, pp. 31–56.

5. *Interpreter's Bible* (New York: Abington, 1956), vol. 5, p. 768.

6. See also Ps. 17:8–9, 36:7, 61:4, 91:4; Ruth 2:12.

7. Mollenkott, *The Divine Feminine*, pp. 92–94.

8. See also Isa. 66:9; Trible, *God and the Rhetoric of Sexuality*, pp. 37–38; and Mollenkott, *The Divine Feminine*, pp. 32–35.

9. The divine name "El Shaddai" appears six times in Genesis, in Exod. 6:3, twice in Numbers 24, twice in Psalms, in Isa. 13:6, in Joel 1:15, twice in Ezekiel, twice in Ruth, and thirty-one times in Job.

10. Trible, *God and the Rhetoric of Sexuality*, p. 61.

11. David Biale, "El Shaddai in the Bible," *History of Religions* 21 (February 1982), pp. 243, 256.

12. Swidler, *Biblical Affirmations of Woman*, pp. 36–39.

13. God is called "Holy One of Israel" also in 2 Kings 19:22; Ps. 71:22, 78:41, 89:18; Isa. 1:4, 5:19, 5:24, 10:20, 12:6, 29:19, 30:11, 30:12, 30:15, 31:1, 37:23, 41:16, 41:20, 43:14, 45:11, 47:4, 48:7, 54:5, 55:5, 60:9, 60:14; Jer. 50:29, 51:5; Ezek. 39:7.

14. God is designated "Holy One" also in Job 6:10; Isa. 10:17, 29:23, 40:25, 43:15, 49:7; Hos. 11:9; Hab. 1:12, 3:3.

15. "Rock" as a metaphor for God also occurs in Ps. 18:31, 18:46, 19:14, 28:1, 31:2, 42:9, 62:2, 62:6, 62:7, 71:3, 78:35, 89:26, 92:15, 94:22, 95:1, 144:1; Isa. 17:10, 51:1.

16. See also Isa. 9:2, 60:20. Rev. 21:23–24 speaks of the fulfillment of this Isaian prophecy.

17. See also Luke 13:34.

18. Hos. 11:1–11; Isa. 49:15, 63:15, 66:13.

19. F. R. Webber, *Church Symbolism*, 2nd ed. (Cleveland: J. H. Jansen, 1938), p. 62.

20. See also Matt. 13:31–33.

21. Robert Hamerton-Kelly, *God the Father: Theology and Patriarchy in the Teaching of Jesus* (Philadelphia: Fortress Press, 1979), pp. 65–81, 101.

22. Ibid., p. 103. For a more thorough understanding of the context, see Hamerton-Kelly's complete discussion in *God the Father*.

23. See also Mark 15:40-41; Matt. 27:55–56.

24. See also John 4:7–26.

25. See also Mark 16:1–7; Luke 24:1–11; John 20:11–17.

26. F. Crawford Burkitt, *Early Eastern Christianity: St. Margaret's Lectures 1904 on the Syriac-Speaking Church* (London: John Murray, 1904), p. 88.

27. For other new birth images, see John 1:13; Gal. 4:28–31; 1 Pet. 1:23; 1 John 2:29, 3:9, 4:7, 5:4, 5:18.

28. See also Col. 2:3; 1 Cor. 1:30.

29. Alan Richardson, *A Theological Word Book of the Bible* (New York: Macmillan, 1950), p. 283.

30. See also John 9:5; 12:46.

Chapter 3: How We Got Where We Are

1. Justin, *The First Apology of Justin Martyr*, trans. John Kaye (Edinburgh: John Grant, 1912), pp. 11–12.

2. Clement of Alexandria, *Paedagogus, The Ante-Nicene Fathers: The Writings of the Fathers down to A.D. 325*, ed. Alexander Roberts and James Donaldson, vol. 2 (New York: Charles Scribner's Sons, 1908), pp. 220–221.

3. Origen, *Commentary on John, The Ante-Nicene Fathers: The Writings of the Fathers down to A.D. 325*, ed. Allan Menzies, vol. 9 (New York: Christian Literature Company, 1896), pp. 317–318.

4. Ambrose, *The Sacrament of the Incarnation of Our Lord, Theological and Dogmatic Works*, trans. Roy J. Deferrari (Washington: The Catholic University of America Press, 1963), p. 223.

5. Augustine, *On the Trinity, Basic Writings of Saint Augustine*, ed. Whitney J. Oates, vol. 2 (New York: Random House, 1948), book XII, V, p. 811.

6. Ibid.

7. Augustine, *Sermons on New-Testament Lessons, Nicene and Post-Nicene Fathers of the Christian Church*, ed. Philip Schaff, vol. 6 (New York: Christian Literature Company, 1888), Sermon LV, p. 434.

8. Caroline Walker Bynum, *Jesus as Mother: Studies in the Spirituality of the High Middle Ages* (Berkeley: University of California Press,

1982), pp. 129-135. See Bynum's thorough explanation of maternal imagery for God in medieval literature in chapter 4, pp. 110-169.

9. Anselm, *Proslogium; Monologium; An Appendix in Behalf of the Fool by Gaunilon; and Cur Deus Homo*, trans. Sidney Norton Deane (La Salle, Ill.: Open Court, 1951), chapter 62, p. 105.

10. Anselm, "Oratio LXV ad Sanctum Paulum Apostolum," *Opera Omnia, Patrologia Latina*, ed. J. P. Migne, vol. 158 (Paris, 1863), cols. 981-982.

11. Bernard, *On the Song of Songs 1, The Works of Bernard of Clairvaux*, trans. Kilian Walsh (Spencer, Mass.: Cistercian Publishers, 1971), Sermon 9, p. 56.

12. Bernard, *St. Bernard of Clairvaux: Seen through His Selected Letters*, trans. Bruno Scott James (Chicago: Henry Regnery Company, 1953), p. 254.

13. Bonaventure, *The Mystical Vine, The Works of Bonaventure*, trans. Jose de Vinck (Paterson, N.J.: St. Anthony Guild Press, 1960), pp. 188-189.

14. Bonaventure, *Journey of the Mind to God, The Works of Bonaventure*, trans. Jose de Vinck (Paterson, N.J.: St. Anthony Guild Press, 1960), p. 46.

15. St. Thomas Aquinas, *Summa Theologiae*, trans. Herbert McCabe (London: Blackfriars, 1964), vol. 3, 1a, 13, 1, p. 49.

16. Aquinas, trans. Edmund Hill, vol. 13, 1a, 12, 1, p. 37.

17. Aquinas, trans. R. J. Batten, vol. 34, 2a, 23, 2, p. 13.

18. Julian of Norwich, *Revelations of Divine Love*, ed. Dom Roger Hudleston (London: Burns & Oates, 1927), p. 119.

19. Ibid., pp. 121-122.

20. Ibid., pp. 123-131.

21. Martin Luther, *Lectures on Genesis, Chapters 1-5*, ed. Jaroslav Pelikan, *Luther's Works*, ed. Jaroslav Pelikan, vol. 1 (St. Louis: Concordia, 1958), p. 11.

22. Ibid., p. 9.

23. Luther, *Lectures on Isaiah, Chapters 40-66*, ed. Hilton C. Oswald, *Luther's Works*, vol. 17 (St. Louis: Concordia, 1972), pp. 139, 183, 410.

24. Ulrich Zwingli, "Exposition of the Christian Faith," *On Providence and Other Essays*, ed. William John Hinke (Durham, N.C.: Labyrinth Press, 1922), p. 238.

25. Zwingli, "An Account of the Faith of Zwingli," ibid., p. 36.

26. Menno Simons, *Confession of the Triune God: The Complete Writings of Menno Simons*, ed. J. C. Wenger, trans. Leonard Verduin (Scottdale, Pa.: Herald Press, 1956), p. 491.

27. John Calvin, *Institutes of the Christian Religion*, ed. John T. McNeill, trans. Ford Lewis Battles, vol. 1 (Philadelphia: Westminster Press, 1969), book 1, chapter 10, p. 100.

28. Calvin, *Commentary on the Book of the Prophet Isaiah*, trans.

William Pringle, vol. 3 (Grand Rapids: Eerdmans, 1948), pp. 302, 303, 436.

29. Calvin, *Commentary on the Book of the Prophet Isaiah,* trans. William Pringle, vol. 4 (Edinburgh: Calvin Translation Society, 1853), p. 30.

30. Friedrich Schleiermacher, *The Christian Faith* (Edinburgh: T. & T. Clark, 1928), pp. 211, 230.

31. Søren Kierkegaard, *Christian Discourses,* trans. Walter Lowrie (London: Oxford University Press, 1939), pp. 298–300.

32. Kierkegaard, "Two Discourses at the Communion on Fridays," *A Kierkegaard Anthology,* ed. Robert Bretall (Princeton, N.J.: Princeton University Press, 1946), pp. 423–424.

33. Karl Barth, *The Knowledge of God and the Service of God According to the Teaching of the Reformation,* trans. J.L.M. Haire and Ian Henderson (London: Hodder and Stoughton, 1938), pp. 31, 33.

34. Ibid., pp. 33–34.

35. Barth, *The Doctrine of the Word of God,* trans. G. T. Thomson, *Church Dogmatics,* vol. 1 (Edinburgh: T. & T. Clark, 1936), p. 2.

36. Paul Tillich, *Systematic Theology,* vol. 3 (Chicago: University of Chicago Press, 1963), p. 293.

37. Ibid., p. 294.

38. Ibid.

Chapter 4: Models of Change

1. *Words That Hurt and Words That Heal: Language About God and People* (Nashville: United Methodist Publishing House, 1985), p. 15.

2. Augustine, *The Trinity,* trans. Stephen McKenna (Washington: Catholic University of America Press, 1963), p. 236.

3. See discussions of Prov. 1 and 8 and Hos. 13:8 in chapter 2. See also Luke 15:3–7, 11–24, and Isa. 40:11 for tender, nurturing masculine pictures of God. The Good Shepherd image of God and Christ suggests traits traditionally labelled feminine as much or more so than those labelled masculine.

4. Dallas M. Roark, *The Christian Faith: An Introduction to Christian Thought* (Grand Rapids: Baker Book House, 1969), pp. 127–128.

5. James Oliver Buswell, *A Systematic Theology of the Christian Religion* (Grand Rapids: Zondervan, 1962), Part 3, p. 47.

6. See comments on Genesis 1:27 in chapter 2.

7. Buswell, *A Systematic Theology of the Christian Religion,* Part 1, p. 119.

8. Edmund J. Fortman, *The Triune God: A Historical Study of the Doctrine of the Trinity* (London: Hutchinson, 1972), pp. 63, 66–68.

9. *Documents of the Christian Church,* ed. Henry Bettenson (London: Oxford University Press, 1963), p. 26.

10. Fortman, *The Triune God*, p. 63.

11. Mary Daly, "After the Death of God the Father," in *Womanspirit Rising*, ed. Carol P. Christ and Judith Plaskow (San Francisco: Harper & Row, 1979), p. 56.

12. Sharon Neufer Emswiler and Thomas Neufer Emswiler, *Women and Worship* (San Francisco: Harper & Row, 1974), p. 8.

Chapter 5: God-Language and Self-Esteem in Women

1. *Children's Letters to God*, compiled by Eric Marshall and Stuart Hample (New York: Simon and Schuster, 1966), n.p.

2. Miriam Greenspan, *A New Approach to Women and Therapy* (New York: McGraw-Hill, 1983), p. 30.

3. Carol Gilligan, *In a Different Voice* (Cambridge: Harvard University Press, 1982), p. 2.

4. Sharon Neufer Emswiler and Thomas Neufer Emswiler, *Women and Worship* (San Francisco: Harper & Row, 1974), pp. 3–4.

5. Linda Tschirhart Sanford and Mary Ellen Donovan, *Women and Self-Esteem* (New York: Penguin Books, 1985), p. 165.

6. This narrative and others in the chapter are based on interviews. People are designated by pseudonyms, not by their real names.

7. Gastroplasty is the surgical stapling of a portion of the upper stomach to create a pouch that holds one to two ounces of food at a time. The purpose of the surgery is weight loss due to drastic reduction in the amount of food intake.

8. Sara Maitland, *A Map of the New Country: Women and Christianity* (London: Routledge and Kegan Paul, 1983), p. 177.

9. These quotations are responses to the question on the Religious Opinion survey: "How would you feel if God were called 'She' as well as 'He,' 'Mother' as well as 'Father'?" (See Appendix A.)

10. Elinor Lenz and Barbara Myerhoff, *The Feminization of America* (Los Angeles: Jeremy P. Tarcher, 1985), p. 139.

11. The conclusions concerning the relationship between gender concepts of God and personality traits are drawn from surveying 174 people, 117 women and 57 men. This sample, from six Christian denominations, volunteered to participate in a survey that included two instruments: a religious survey that I designed to determine gender concepts of God (survey included in Appendix A); and "The Adjective Check List," by Harrison G. Gough (Berkeley: University of California). From the religious survey, respondents were placed in two categories: androgynous or transcendent God and masculine God (scheme for classification into the two categories included in Appendix A). t tests were then run to compare the mean scores for the two categories on the following ten scales of the Adjective Check List: achievement, dominance, nurturance, autonomy, aggression, change, abasement, def-

erence, self-confidence, and creative personality. For technical statistical analysis, see Appendix B. Interpretations of scores are based on *The Adjective Check List Manual*, by Harrison G. Gough and Alfred B. Heilbrun (Palo Alto, Calif.: Consulting Psychologists Press, 1983).

12. These quotations are responses to the question on the religious survey: "How do you feel in a worship service in which all references to God are masculine?"

13. M. Scott Peck, *The Road Less Traveled* (New York: Simon and Schuster, 1978), p. 82.

14. Sanford and Donovan, *Women and Self-Esteem*, p. 3.

15. This is one response to the question on the religious survey: "How do you feel in a worship service in which all references to God are masculine?"

16. See chapter 1, page 10 above, for a discussion of the feminine Spirit (*Ruach*) in the Hebrew Bible.

Chapter 6: God-Language and Spirituality in Men

1. Mark Gerzon, *A Choice of Heroes: The Changing Faces of American Manhood* (Boston: Houghton Mifflin, 1982), p. 229.

2. Gail Sheehy, *Pathfinders* (New York: Bantam, 1981), p. 237.

3. National Center for Health Statistics: *Health, U.S., 1988*, DHHS Pub. No. (PHS) 89-1232, Public Health Service, Washington, U.S. Government Printing Office, March 1989, p. 53. *Statistical Abstract of the United States*, 108th edition (Washington: U.S. Bureau of the Census, 1988), pp. 81.

4. David R. Mace, *Close Companions* (New York: Continuum, 1982). In Part One, pp. 3–57, Mace contrasts the traditional hierarchical and the companionship, or partnership, marriage, advocating the latter for the highest level of love and intimacy.

5. Dorothy Dinnerstein, *The Mermaid and the Minotaur: Sexual Arrangements and the Human Malaise* (San Francisco: Harper & Row, 1963), p. 200.

6. Gerzon, *A Choice of Heroes*, pp. 223–224. Gerzon gives one of the most convincing arguments for changing patriarchal images of God for men's sake.

7. Sara Maitland, *A Map of the New Country: Women and Christianity* (London: Routledge and Kegan Paul, 1983), p. 189.

8. A survey conducted by Louis Harris revealed that 46 percent of American women and only 33 percent of American men are regular in church attendance. See *Inside America* (New York: Random House, 1987), p. 68.

9. Gerzon, *A Choice of Heroes*, p. 222.

10. This narrative and others in the chapter are based on interviews. People are designated by pseudonyms, not by their real names.

11. See chapter 5, note 11 above, for a description of the research upon which these conclusions are based. The linking of men's attitudes toward the gender of God and the equality of women is based on the finding that 97 percent of the men in the sample with androgynous or gender-transcendent concepts of God were in favor of ordained female ministers.

12. Roger A. Paynter, "God-Talk," unpublished sermon (October 27, 1985).

13. No one in the entire sample of 174 conceived God as exclusively feminine.

14. Elinor Lenz and Barbara Myerhoff, *The Feminization of America* (Los Angeles: Jeremy P. Tarcher, 1985), p. 143.

15. See note 8 above. Also my research sample suggests that men are less actively involved in church than women. I went to Bible study, theological study, and prayer groups, seeking equal numbers of women and men to survey. Almost 100 percent of those present volunteered to participate in the survey. A little over twice as many women as men attended these groups, resulting in my sample of 57 men and 117 women.

16. Sharon Neufer Emswiler and Thomas Neufer Emswiler, *Women and Worship* (San Franscisco: Harper & Row, 1974), p. xi.

Chapter 7: God-Language and the Church's Future

1. Sara Maitland, *A Map of the New Country: Women and Christianity* (London: Routledge and Kegan Paul, 1983), p. 188.

2. Paul Jewett, *The Ordination of Women* (Grand Rapids: Eerdmans, 1980), p. 101.

3. These percentages are based on responses to my religious opinion survey. Chi-square tests were run to compare the two categories (androgynous or transcendent God and masculine God) according to their responses concerning the ordination of women and women as pastors/priests.

It may be surprising to some that of this sample of people in a Central Texas city in the traditional "Bible Belt," 80 percent believe that churches should ordain women, and 81 percent believe that women should have opportunities to serve as pastors/priests. In the Roman Catholic sample 56 percent believe in the ordination of women. Perhaps the pope underestimates the support for women priests.

4. "Declaration on the Question of the Admission of Women to the Ministerial Priesthood," *Vatican Council II: More Postconciliar Documents*, ed. Austin Flannery (Collegeville, Minn.: Liturgical Press, 1982), p. 339.

5. See chapter 7, "Energizing the Grass Roots," in Kanter's *The Change Masters* (New York: Simon and Schuster, 1983), pp. 180–205.

Kanter says that the participative organizational structure is also more integrative and change-oriented than the hierarchical organization.

6. Maitland, *A Map of the New Country*, p. 26. See also Lenz and Myerhoff, *The Feminization of America* (Los Angeles: Jeremy P. Tarcher, 1985), pp. 57–74, for similar ideas on the advantages of the feminine style of networking.

7. "Prescott Memorial calls Nancy Sehested as Senior Pastor," *SBC Today*, October 1987, p. 5.

8. Susan Weidman Schneider, *Jewish and Female* (New York: Simon and Schuster, 1984), p. 80. See also Rita M. Gross, "Female God Language in a Jewish Context," in *Womanspirit Rising* (San Francisco: Harper & Row, 1979), p. 167.

9. Lenz and Myerhoff, *The Feminization of America*, p. 139.

10. Rom. 12:6; 1 Cor. 12:31.

Epilogue: Beyond God as Male and Female

1. For over ten years generic language has been passing out of standard English usage. Professional journals in the behavioral sciences will not publish articles that do not use inclusive language. The National Council of Teachers of English recommends avoiding generic pronouns "to avoid the impression that every person is a 'he.'" This group of language authorities gives two options for avoiding masculine pronouns to refer to singular nouns of indefinite sex: (1) alternate the pronoun gender, using "she" in one paragraph and "he" in another; (2) use "he or she" as a single reference (Anne Agee and Gary Kline, *The Basic Writer's Book*, 2nd ed. [Englewood Cliffs, N.J.: Prentice-Hall, 1981], p. 123).

When it is necessary to use pronouns to refer to God, I advocate a similar balancing of gender references.

Inclusive Language Resources for the Church

Carlisle, Thomas John. *Eve and After: Old Testament Women in Portrait*. Grand Rapids: Eerdmans, 1984.

Carlisle, Thomas John. *Beginning with Mary: Women of the Gospels in Portrait*. Grand Rapids: Eerdmans, 1986.

Duck, Ruth C., and Michael G. Brausch. *Everflowing Streams: Songs for Worship*. New York: Pilgrim Press, 1981.

Duck, Ruth C., ed. *Bread for the Journey: Resources for Worship*. New York: Pilgrim Press, 1981.

Emswiler, Sharon Neufer, and Thomas Neufer Emswiler, eds. *Sisters and Brothers Sing!* 2nd ed. Normal, Ill.: Wesley Foundation, 1977.

Emswiler, Thomas Neufer, and Sharon Neufer Emswiler. *Wholeness in Worship: Creative Models for Sunday, Family, and Special Services*. San Francisco: Harper & Row, 1980.

Emswiler, Sharon Neufer, and Thomas Neufer Emswiler. *Women and Worship*. San Francisco: Harper & Row, 1974.

Hardesty, Nancy A. *Inclusive Language in the Church*. Atlanta: John Knox Press, 1987.

Huber, Jane Parker. *Joy in Singing*. Atlanta: Office of Women and Joint Office of Worship of the Presbyterian Church, 1983.

Huber, Jane Parker. *A Singing Faith*. Philadelphia: Westminster, 1987.

An Inclusive Language Lectionary: Readings for Years A–C. Division of Education and Ministry, National Council of Churches of Christ in the U.S.A. Published for the Cooperative Publication Association by John Knox Press, Atlanta; Pilgrim Press, New York; Westminster Press, Philadelphia; 1983.

Miller, Casey, and Kate Swift. *The Handbook of Nonsexist Writing*. New York: Lippincott and Crowell, 1980.

Ruether, Rosemary Radford. *Sexism and God-Talk: Toward a Feminist Theology*. Boston: Beacon Press, 1983.

Russell, Letty, M., ed. *The Liberating Word: A Guide to Non-Sexist Interpretation of the Bible.* Philadelphia: Westminster, 1976.

Schaffran, Janet, and Pat Kozak. *More Than Words: Prayer and Ritual for Inclusive Communities.* Bloomington, Ind.: Meyer-Stone Books, 1986.

The United Methodist Hymnal. Nashville: United Methodist Publishing House, 1988. Includes new hymns with inclusive images of God and changes some traditional hymns to make language inclusive.

Watkins, Keith. *Faithful and Fair: Transcending Sexist Language in Worship.* Nashville: Abingdon, 1981.

Winter, Miriam Therese. *WomanPrayer, WomanSong.* Bloomington, Ind.: Meyer-Stone Books, 1987.

Words That Hurt and Words That Heal: Language About God and People. Nashville: United Methodist Publishing House, 1985.

Wren, Brian. *What Language Shall I Borrow? God Talk in Worship: A Male Response to Feminist Theology.* New York: Crossroad and London: SCM Press, 1989.

Index of Scripture References

GENESIS
1, *23*
1:1, *117*
1:1–2, *10*
1:2, *22*
1:26, *22*
1:27, *22, 41, 121*
49:25, *27*

EXODUS
6:3, *118*
19:4, *118*
20:4, *21*
20:17, *16*
33:19, *23*

NUMBERS
5:11–31, *10*
24, *118*
27:1–11, *10*
30:3–15, *10*

DEUTERONOMY
32:11, *22*
32:11–12, *20, 24, 64*

RUTH
2:12, *118*

1 SAMUEL
21, *9*

2 SAMUEL
10:18, *9*

2 KINGS
19:22, *118*

1 CHRONICLES
19:18, *9*

JOB
6:10, *118*

PSALMS
17:8–9, *118*
18:2, *29*
18:31, *118*
18:46, *118*
19:1, *7*
19:14, *118*
22:9–10, *26*
27:1, *29, 35*
28:1, *118*
31:2, *118*
31:3, *29*
36:7, *118*
42:9, *118*
57:1, *26*
61:4, *118*
62:2, *118*
62:2a, *29*
62:6, *118*
62:7, *118*
71:3, *118*
71:22, *118*
78:35, *118*
78:41, *28, 118*
79:6, *10*

PSALMS (cont.)
89:18, *118*
89:26, *118*
91:4, *118*
92:15, *118*
94:22, *29, 118*
95:1, *118*
123:2, *26*
137, *5*
144:1, *118*

PROVERBS
1, *121*
1:20, *27*
1:23, *27*
1:33, *27*
4:5b–6, *28*
4:8–9, *28*
4:11, *34*
4:22, *34*
4:26, *34*
8, *121*
8:22–31, *34*

ISAIAH
1:4, *118*
5:19, *118*
5:24, *118*
9:2, *118*
10:17, *118*
10:20, *118*
12:6, *118*
13:6, *118*
17:7, *28*
17:10, *118*
26:4, *29*
29:19, *118*
29:23, *118*
30:11, *118*
30:12, *118*
30:15, *118*
31:1, *118*
37:23, *118*

40:11, *121*
40:25, *28, 118*
41:14b, *28*
41:16, *118*
41:20, *118*
42:13, *24*
42:14, *24, 49*
43:3, *28*
43:14, *118*
43:15, *28, 118*
45:11, *118*
46:3, *47, 49*
46:3–4, *25*
47:4, *118*
48:7, *118*
49:15, *25, 47, 119*
51:1, *118*
54:5, *118*
55:5, *118*
55:8, *108*
55:8–9, *5*
60:9, *118*
60:14, *118*
60:19, *29*
60:20, *118*
63, *24*
63:15, *119*
63:15–16, *25*
66:9, *118*
66:13, *17, 26, 47, 119*

JEREMIAH
31:20, *118*
50:29, *118*
51:5, *118*

EZEKIEL
39:7, *118*

HOSEA
11:1–11, *119*
11:3, *24*
11:8, *24*

11:9, *118*
13:8, *24, 121*

JOEL
1:15, *118*

HABAKKUK
1:12, *118*
3:3, *118*

MATTHEW
5:13–14, *79*
5:30, *41*
5:44, *5*
6:9, *15, 31*
10:37, *32*
13:31–33, *119*
16:25, *76*
19:6, *13*
19:12, *41*
19:19, *78*
23:37, *20, 30, 43*
25:14–30, *78*
27:5, *9*
27:55–56, *119*
28:1–8, *33*

MARK
2:26, *9*
15:40–41, *119*
16:1–7, *119*

LUKE
4:18, *17*
7:34–35, *35*
8:1–3, *32*
10:38–41, *33*
11:49, *34*
13:18–21, *31*
13:34, *118*
15, *16*
15:1–10, *30*
15:3–7, *121*

15:11–14, *121*
24:1–11, *119*

JOHN
1:1, *35*
1:3, *35*
1:4–5, *35*
1:9, *35*
1:13, *119*
3:6, *34*
3:8, *7*
4:7–26, *119*
4:24, *62*
6:35, *36*
6:48, *36*
6:51, *36*
6:51–57, *36*
8:12, *35*
8:32, *17*
9:5, *119*
10:9, *36*
12:46, *119*
14:6, *34, 36*
14:26, *33, 60*
16:12, *8, 11*
16:21, *6*
20:11–17, *119*

ACTS
1:18, *9*
15:1, *10*

ROMANS
1:20, *7*
12:3, *81*
12:6, *125*

1 CORINTHIANS
1:30, *119*
2:10, *7*
8:13, *79*
12:7–14, *99*
12:31, *125*

2 CORINTHIANS
1:23–24, *34*
4:6, *35*
5:17–19, *34*

GALATIANS
3:28, *8, 39, 95*
4:28–31, *119*

EPHESIANS
4:11, *96*
6:5, *10*

COLOSSIANS
1:15–17, *35*
2:3, *119*

1 TIMOTHY
2:9, *14*
2:11–12, *14*
2:15, *14*

2 TIMOTHY
3:16, *6*

1 PETER
1:23, *119*

1 JOHN
1, *59*
2:29, *119*
3:9, *119*
4:2–3, *59*
4:7, *119*
4:19, *78*
5:4, *119*
5:18, *119*

REVELATION
21:5, *3*
21:23–24a, *36*
21:23–24, *118*

General Index

Abba, 15, 31, 32
Adoptionism, 58, 59, 61
Agee, Ann, 125
Ambrose, St., 41, 54, 108, 119
Anselm of Canterbury, St., 38, 43, 44, 54, 120
Aquinas, St. Thomas, 39, 44, 45, 59, 120
Arian heresy, 41
Arianism, 41, 60, 61
Augustine, St., 39, 41, 42, 45, 46, 55, 56, 119, 121

Barth, Karl, 51, 52, 53, 54, 121
Bernard of Clairvaux, 44, 120
Bettenson, Henry, 121
Biale, David, 118
biblical inspiration, 5, 6, 9
biblical interpretation, 6
biblical translation, 6
Bonaventure, St., 44, 120
Burkitt, F. Crawford, 119
Buswell, James Oliver, 121
Bynum, Caroline Walker, 119

Caldicott, Dr. Helen, 104
Calvin, John, 48, 49, 54, 59, 120, 121
Church Women United, 102
Clement of Alexandria, 40, 54, 119
Council of Nicea, 60

Daly, Mary, 63, 122

Dinnerstein, Dorothy, 83, 123
Docetism, 59, 61
Donovan, Mary Ellen, 68, 69, 122, 123
dynamic theory, 9

Ebionism, 58, 59, 61
El Shaddai, 27
Elohim, 21
Erikson, Erik, 67
Evangelical Women's Caucus, 102

Fielding, Dr. Wanda, 70
Fortman, Edmund J., 121, 122
Freud, Sigmund, 67

Gerzon, Mark, 81, 123
Gilligan, Carol, 67, 122
Gough, Harrison G., 111, 122
Greenspan, Miriam, 122
Gross, Rita M., 125

Hamerton-Kelly, Robert, 119
Hample, Stuart, 122
Harris, Louis, 123
Hastings, Rev. Deborah, 71
Heilbrun, Alfred B., 123

hermeneutics, 15–16
Holland, Rev. Patricia Gladney, 17, 118

inspiration, 7–9

133

James I, King, 12
Jerome, 11
Jerusalem Bible, 13
Jewett, Paul, 96, 124
Julian of Norwich, 45, 46, 120
Justin Martyr, 40, 119

Kanter, Rosabeth Moss, 99, 124
Kierkegaard, Søren, 50, 51, 121
King James Version, 13, 14
Kline, Gary, 125
Kohlberg, Lawrence, 67

Lenz, E., 91, 122, 124, 125
Lewis, C. S., 8, 10, 117
Logos, 35, 53
Luther, Martin, 46, 47, 54, 120

Mace, David R., 123
Maitland, Sara, 95, 122, 123,
    124, 125
Manichean philosophy, 41
Marshall, Eric, 122
Mary, 46, 61
mechanical dictation theory, 9
Modalism, 57, 58, 61
Mollenkott, Virginia Ramey,
    118
Moore, Bishop Paul, 83, 94
Myerhoff, B., 91, 122, 124, 125

National Council of Churches,
    12, 107
Neufer Emswiler, Sharon, 68,
    117, 122, 124
Neufer Emswiler, Tom, 92, 117,
    122, 124
Nicene Creed, 60

Origen, 39, 40, 41, 45, 60, 81,
    119

Paynter, Roger A., 124

Peace Links, 104
Peck, Scott, 78, 123
Phillips, John Bertram, 2, 117
Physicians for Social
    Responsibility, 104
Psychologists for Social
    Responsibility, 104

revelation, 7, 8, 10
Revised Standard Version, 12,
    14
Richardson, Alan, 35, 119
Roark, Dallas M., 121
Ruach, 22, 33, 79, 104

Sanford, Linda Tschirhart, 68,
    69, 122, 123
Schleiermacher, Friedrich, 50,
    51, 121
Schneider, Susan Weidman,
    101, 125
Sehested, Nancy, 125
Sheehy, Gail, 123
Simons, Menno, 48, 120
Sophia, 34
Stanton, Elizabeth Cady, 15
Subordinationism, 60, 61
Swidler, Leonard, 118

Teresa, Mother, 98
Tertullian, 39
Tillich, Paul, 42, 53, 54, 108,
    121
Trible, Phyllis, 118
Tyndale, William, 11, 12

verbal plenary theory, 9

Webber, F. R., 119
Wisdom, 27, 34, 35, 41, 42, 43,
    48, 58
Women Strike for Peace, 104

Women's Action for Nuclear
  Disarmament, 104
Women's International League
  for Peace and Freedom, 104
Women's Peace League in
  Europe, 103

World Peacemakers, 104
Wycliffe, John, 11

Zwingli, Ulrich, 47, 48, 120